Ann -

It was great to see you at the reunion. I truly believe that you are among those who have aged the least. Here's a celebration of the present moment for you. I hope you and all your family have a happy next year + rest of your lives.

Thanks + love,

Mike Wolf

12/15/15

A Summary of Buddhadharma

Michael S. Wolf

Worldwinds Communications
Baton Rouge, Louisiana

ISBN: 0615563287
ISBN 13: 9780615563282
Library of Congress Control Number: 2014956212
Worldwinds Communications
P.O. Box 3094, Baton Rouge, LA 70821-3094

This work is dedicated to
Salem Chennafi and Prof. George W. Pugh,
two men worthy of being called educators,
whose benevolent curiosity set the project in motion.

Contents

Part One

Buddhadharma

Buddhadharma is a vast collection of teachings, ideas, and practices designed to expand human awareness and happiness that were formulated by Siddhartha Gautama, called the Buddha (the Enlightened One) and also known as Shakyamuni (the Sage of the Shakyas – from the name of his family clan), in the 6th century BCE. The traditionally transmitted teachings of Buddha were modified and supplemented by his followers over the centuries in many lands. As Buddha transformed the existing philosophy of his time, his successors have altered and elaborated the understanding of Buddhist teachings, generating many local and evolving variations.

Buddhadharma is primarily a set of practices and attitudes. It cannot be reduced exclusively to any concepts or doctrines. This summary is not definitive, but illustrative.

The Five Skandhas

Shakyamuni Buddha and his collaborators analyzed human experience into five component categories called skandhas: form, feelings, perceptions, formation (intentions and actions), and consciousness. By enlightened self-observation, they taught, one can learn the nature of the skandhas and escape serious misunderstandings and sufferings they produce.

Buddhist wisdom consists generally of understanding the actions of the skandhas, especially the skandha of consciousness, which is the main determinant of experienced reality. Buddha taught that enlightenment is the natural condition of the human mind, but that the mind's nature is obscured by disturbing emotions and ideas, and by enduring misconceptions that consciousness tends to generate. Buddhist practice consists of cultivating behaviors that tend to increase accurate and productive understanding of consciousness in oneself and others, and avoiding contrary behaviors that tend to increase confusion and suffering.

The Eight Consciousnesses

Buddhist teachings often subdivide consciousness into eight kinds, corresponding to the principal sensory inputs and mental functions. Thus there are five consciousnesses generated by the physical sense organs: sight, hearing, smell, taste, and touch. The sixth consciousness is the mind of ordinary conception and reflection. The seventh consciousness is the subtle conception of a self, considered the underlying source of most conceptual error. The eighth consciousness is said to be a repository of all mental forces where habitual predispositions, feelings, and ideas generate their associated effects and ensuing states of mind.

The five sensory consciousnesses reflect the physical conditions of sense objects. The sixth consciousness interprets the sensory impressions and produces thought, memory, and imagination. The perceptions and conceptions of the sixth consciousness are called dharmas. The first six consciousnesses or aspects of the mind are therefore the foundation of all experience. The objects of awareness which they apprehend are described respectively as sights, sounds, scents, tastes, tactile feelings, and dharmas. The general classification of all ideas and experiences as dharmas is a powerful concept that calls to mind the common nature of all phenomena.

While Buddhists have articulated and debated many philosophical and psychological propositions over the centuries, their fundamental practice has always been the development of wisdom and compassion in the human mind. The processes by which this mental development can occur are many and often subtle. Though often stimulated and guided by language, action, and logical analysis, these mental experiences largely transcend speech and mental analysis. They can be experienced, but ultimately they cannot be defined or fully expressed in words. The core of buddhadharma is the experience of pure consciousness unobscured by the delusions of ordinary thought. Its language is metaphorical, but its realization is infinite. Proceeding from these premises, the teachings should be contemplated with care and patience.

In addition to its general meaning of an object of consciousness, the word "dharma" carries the more particular meanings of truth, reality, natural law, doctrine, and teaching. In these senses, the teachings of the Buddha and his followers are usually referred to as "Dharma." The word "buddhadharma" designates both the teachings of the Buddha and the experiences of enlightenment and Buddhist practice.

The Two Truths

When considering Buddhist teachings one should always bear in mind the principle of the Two Truths. According to this fundamental principle, the teachings may express either relative (conditional or expedient) truth or absolute (unconditional or ultimate) truth. The ultimate nature of reality cannot be expressed in words. Most statements of Buddhist doctrine are only intended to convey relative truths, truths revealing partial understanding or understanding of certain aspects of experience. The absolute or ultimate nature of reality is beyond formulation. All Buddhist practices and teachings were developed to produce enlightenment. None of the statements or activities of Buddhist teachers, however subtle or profound, are meant to be substitutes for direct experience by the individual of the nature of consciousness.

The Three Jewels

There are many ways to organize and categorize the Buddhist teachings. Like the classifications of skandhas, consciousnesses, and levels of truth, buddhadharma comprises innumerable sets of principles empirically derived by Shakyamuni and his successors to explicate the path to the full understanding of experience. One concept shared by all Buddhists in this regard is that of the Three Jewels.

The Three Jewels are the Buddha, the Dharma, and the Sangha. They are the reliable guides to enlightenment in all times and places. The Buddha is the enlightened mind, embodied by Shakyamuni and all other awakened beings who conceive and realize the full potential of human consciousness. The Dharma is the body of truth and wisdom realized and expressed by the enlightened ones. It includes both the provisional (relative) and the ultimate teachings of the Buddhas. The Sangha is the community of Buddhist practitioners, those who emulate the Buddhas and seek to actualize the Dharma. Sometimes the Sangha is subclassified into persons on different stages of the Buddhist path or persons following different teachers.

The most important point about the Sangha is the implication that buddhadharma is a real human experience that can be realized by all. The collectivity of those who share insight into the true nature of reality is a powerful institution capable of engendering and developing such insight in others. Even in the absence of extraordinarily enlightened teachers like the buddhas, it is always possible to obtain effective Dharma guidance and relief from the bitter sufferings of existence through the kind help of the many selfless, skillful men and women of the Sangha.

It is traditional for persons undertaking to practice buddhadharma to begin by "taking refuge" in the Buddha, the Dharma, and the Sangha, thereby signifying their aspiration to attain enlightenment and to actualize the values represented by the Three Jewels.

The Three Turnings of the Dharma Wheel

As Buddhist teachings evolved, practitioners and scholars classified them into different stages and categories. The earlier teachings always formed the foundation for the later ones, so the earlier ones were generally not repudiated, but rather supplemented and expanded, by the later ones. Eventually many Buddhists came to identify three phases of the Buddha's Dharma, described as three turnings of the wheel of the teaching (dharmachakra). Regardless of historical origins, these phases are convenient categories for exposition.

The First Turning of the Dharma Wheel: the Four Noble Truths and the Noble Eightfold Path

The first turning of the Dharma wheel refers to the earliest teachings of Shakyamuni. These began with the Four Noble Truths Siddhartha taught to his companions soon after experiencing a profound enlightenment during a period of intense meditation, following several years of renunciation and spiritual seeking. Siddhartha had abandoned a privileged life of luxury to study the dynamics of human suffering in hopes of discovering a means of transcending such hardships as sickness, aging, unhappiness, and death. He had separated from his companions in asceticism to pursue a more moderate course of practice, one involving rest and refreshment as well as discipline and concentration (a "Middle Way").

The four truths that Siddhartha taught were:

1. Life is suffering (dukkha).
2. There is an origin of suffering.

3. There is an end of suffering.
4. There is a way to end suffering, namely the Noble Eightfold Path.

The Noble Eightfold Path consists of:

(1) Right understanding
(2) Right intention
(3) Right speech
(4) Right action
(5) Right livelihood
(6) Right effort
(7) Right mindfulness
(8) Right meditation (samadhi).

When Siddhartha explained his newfound truths to his companions, they became so impressed with him that they declared him enlightened and thereafter called him "Buddha." The Four Noble Truths encompass the essence of Buddhist wisdom.

Dukkha, the inevitable suffering of existence, is the fundamental problem of consciousness. The universality of impermanence and change in biological existence inevitably produces suffering and mental anguish for beings, leading into all the worlds of misery that life can generate. For Siddhartha, recognizing that there is an elemental unsatisfactoriness in human existence was the beginning of overcoming it. Siddhartha found the origin of dukkha in the innate tendency of the mind to grasp experienced phenomena as durable realities. Seeing that all dharmas of mental experience were impermanent and conditioned by other thoughts and happenings, Siddhartha refrained from interpreting his ideas and perceptions as lasting or ultimately real. In the state of unbiased perception, with no attempt to interpret experience to fit preconceptions, he found the end of dukkha, an alternative natural state that exposed new dimensions of consciousness, tranquility, and freedom.

Samsara and Nirvana

In Siddhartha's time, life was commonly seen as a succession of births and deaths repeating continually until an individual soul attained union with a universal soul. The cycle of births and deaths was called samsara, a word used to describe the process of ordinary life. The state of peace and liberation discovered by Siddhartha was called nirvana, a word implying the extinction of the personal soul in what could still be called a larger reality, but not a reality personified as a world spirit or being, or even subject to characterization of any kind.

Right Understanding: Emptiness, Dependent Origination, Karma, and Selflessness

The way Siddhartha proposed for liberating oneself from the sufferings of life depended primarily on insight into the nature of experience or apparent reality (dharmas). The most significant aspect of this nature is emptiness (shunyata), an absence of inherent characteristics in a field of consciousness. Emptiness reflects the conditional and ephemeral nature of all phenomena, and the way sensation and thought appear and disappear in the mind. Emptiness can be understood logically and deduced intellectually from experience, but it is known most fully in direct perception of mental and sensory phenomena, achieved by mindful awareness and deliberate meditation (dhyana).

A fundamental causal sequence Siddhartha observed in the formation of mental experience is called dependent origination. He taught that all experience developed from a twelve-step process of perception, interpretation, and reaction involving the following stages (nidanas), called the Twelve Links of Dependent Origination:

1. Unconsciousness
2. Mental action
3. Consciousness
4. Discrimination
5. Sensation and thought
6. Contact
7. Feeling
8. Craving
9. Grasping
10. Existence (becoming)
11. Birth
12. Aging and death.

The twelve nidanas describe both the developmental process by which a human mind is formed and extinguished, and the cognitive process by which a thought originates and ends.

That thought and mentality are conditioned by underlying psychological processes of perception, identification, and objectification, as described by Siddhartha, could be realized by reflection and meditation, and was confirmed by his followers. Those who persistently studied their minds saw that all aspects of life are impermanent and conditionally determined. They saw how mental assumptions and experiences generate successive ideas and actions. Essentially, all phenomena prove to be interdependent. This being, that happens; this ceasing, that stops.

Analyzing the causal conditions of things reveals that nothing exists independently and permanently. Everything depends on the conditions and causal chains producing it. All observations and all ideas depend on the conditions of perception and conception involved. Seeing the dependence of thought and experience on constantly changing conditions, Siddhartha called the nature of human experience "empty."

The Four Noble Truths, the Noble Eightfold Path, and the teachings on dependent origination illustrate Buddha's emphasis on the practicalities of causation (karma). In the Buddha's time, every action was considered to include its resulting effects. The word "karma" indicated this joining of cause and effect in all actions. Seen as the results of mental actions, all states of mind might theoretically be traced to their karmic origins, if there weren't too many causes to know.

The Buddha's path was taught to lead people toward understanding emptiness and the causal patterns generated by their minds. The "right understanding" Buddha taught as the first step in his eightfold path meant the accurate understanding of one's own mind. Known as impermanent and conditioned on mental actions, mind was revealed as empty and formless but also infinite in possibilities and manifestations. Neither language nor conception could describe or identify the entire nature of mind, yet its most lasting qualities were always present and active.

Central to the experience of emptiness was the non-existence of a permanent self or soul of any kind. Selflessness was both the philosophical and the practical heart of the Buddha's teaching. Any form of dukkha could be dissolved by asking oneself, "Who is suffering?" Experiencing their minds as selfless emptiness of infinite potential, the Sangha practiced mindful action and contemplation in the spirit of the Buddha's Eightfold Path.

The Buddha taught his path to increase human understanding and happiness. None of his philosophy, however profound, was asserted to be absolute truth. The Buddha often cautioned against taking words as reality and advised his followers to believe none of his Dharma on authority alone, but to accept his teachings only if the individual found them to be true and useful in his own experience.

The concept of emptiness was elaborated further in the Buddha's second turning of the wheel of Dharma as well as in the teachings of many generations of eminent meditators and scholars over the centuries.

The "right understanding" the Buddha taught included understanding the realities of impermanence, dukkha, causation, emptiness, and selflessness. One developing right understanding had to have such an objective and discerning view of human life in order to be capable of realizing the underlying nature of mind and the way to nirvana.

Right Intention

The second aspect of the Buddha's path was right intention (sometimes translated as "right thought"). The consequences of actions are heavily influenced by the intentions with which the actions are done. Intentionality is the essence of the skandha of formation. When physical and mental conditions make fulfillment of our intentions in acting impossible, the karma of our intentions remains active. Good intentions can moderate the effects of bad actions and enhance the effects of good actions. Bad intentions similarly condition the consequences of actions negatively.

In buddhadharma the power of intention is added to all actions and ideas. If one's intentions are to do good, to reduce suffering for oneself and others, and to arrive at a full realization of the Buddha's path, then the intended goals will tend to be realized. In pursuing self-discipline and the cultivation of virtue and understanding, the qualities of the practitioner's intentions never cease to condition his development.

Right Speech, Right Action, and Right Livelihood

Right speech, right action, and right livelihood define in general the moral dimension of the Buddha's path, the way to ethical living. Shakyamuni taught that conduct was virtuous if it increased the happiness and benefit of other beings, or if it prevented injury or suffering for them. He taught that selfless love and compassion should guide our behavior in all circumstances. In the Buddhist tradition, love seeks the happiness of others, while compassion seeks to relieve them of suffering.

Actions of body, speech, and mind derive their moral quality from the consequences they produce and from the intentions with which they are done. Speech should be truthful, helpful, and kind. It should not be deceitful, hurtful, or angry. Actions of all kinds should be motivated by benevolence and cause no harm to anyone. Emphasizing always the causal effects of human action, the Buddha admonished his followers not only to avoid direct injury to beings, but also to avoid creating any conditions that might in the future occasion suffering for them.

Siddhartha's eight-part path was both practical and idealistic. In enjoining his Sangha to penetrate the deeply rooted illusions of human consciousness and to reform their minds, their intentions, and their actions so as to generate selfless compassion and extreme altruism, he was constructing personal and ethical ideals very difficult of attainment. Nevertheless the means he taught for accomplishing the conquest of dukkha were eminently practical, describing step by step, and with alternatives suitable for different aptitudes and personalities, how ordinary people could gradually diminish their mental confusion and uncover the healing inner reality of their lives, where pain and selfish delusion could not exist.

Reflecting the practical cast of his teachings, the fifth part of Siddhartha's path was right livelihood. The many patterns of actions constituting an occupation or livelihood condition substantially the experiences and mentality of the individual and have far-reaching impacts on his family, his associates, and his society. Drawing attention to these sorts of consequences, Siddhartha taught that those seeking moral excellence and enlightenment should pursue honest, constructive occupations that are beneficial to others and not harmful or morally corrupting. One should not, for example, gain his living by theft, fraud, or violence, or by encouraging others to engage in immorality. Offering to injure people for hire, or inducing others to do so; misleading, cheating, or abusing customers, employers, or employees – all such activities would constitute immoral livelihoods bearing adverse karmic consequences. According to Shakyamuni's Dharma, no aspect of life could be separated from its karmic effects.

Engaging in hatred and injury of others always produces damaging repercussions in the minds of wrongdoers as well as in their outer world, rendering the attainment of selfless insight and enlightenment impossible for them. Causing suffering through evil actions and intentions in commerce and public affairs is no less crippling morally and psychologically than the direct infliction of injury in one's personal and family relationships. The Buddha's teaching imposes on the individual complete responsibility for all of his thoughts, words, and deeds. There is no way, the Buddha taught, for anyone to escape the consequences of his ideas and his behavior, just as there is no way that anyone can escape the effects of past causes determining the actual conditions of his life.

Imbued with infinite love and compassion for all beings, the Buddha did not present his teachings in order to judge or condemn those who failed to practice virtuous living. He taught right speech, conduct, lifestyle, and intention in order to rescue the unfortunate and immoral from the misery to which their actions condemned them and to demonstrate the means by which they could transform their lives and establish the conditions of peace and happiness.

The Buddha and his followers illustrated the details of right living through the personal examples of their own behavior. The Buddhist scriptures and literature of all eras and regions are filled with innumerable stories and admonitions describing the moral discipline of the enlightened ones and the means by which they cultivated universal love and boundless devotion to the well-being of all.

Right Effort

The sixth subdivision of the Noble Eightfold Path is right effort. Those seeking to overcome the pervasive miseries of samsara must be willing to work indefatigably toward that goal.

The causes of ignorance, selfishness, and evil are so deeply rooted in human thought and age-old mental and behavioral habits that great and persistent effort is required to overcome them. Without ongoing effort to practice dharma, the illusions of ordinary consciousness and the results of self-centered behavior will continually manifest in our minds. When these forces dominate the personality, even if they are occasionally interrupted by insightful and selfless behavior, the negative influences will tend to resume their prominence when the beneficial states of mind have passed.

Right effort is needed with every part of the eightfold path. The effectiveness of any dharma practice is proportionate to the effort applied by the practitioner.

Right effort does not mean only intense effort. In the Middle Way of the Buddha, timely moderation and relaxation can be as important as force and persistence. Misled by our predispositions and misconceptions, we may fall into errors of excess or overdoing on the dharma path, as in "not seeing the forest for the trees." Ideally, right effort is always appropriately modulated according to the inner and outer circumstances of the practitioner.

While right effort is needed in all dharma practice, it is especially relevant to the practices of mindfulness and meditation because these crucial parts of the path are so easily avoided without deliberate efforts to practice them.

Right Mindfulness

The most essential practice of the Buddhist path is mindfulness, which implies awareness of the conditions and actions of one's own mind as well as those generating the appearances of external phenomena. The transforming discoveries made by Siddhartha originated in the careful observation of his own mind, combined with a perceptive and sympathetic attention to the causes producing the painful experiences of human life.

Right mindfulness is always being alert to what is happening in one's mind – seeing clearly the perceptions, reflections, and reactions one makes in the course of daily life and ultimately in all moments of consciousness. This kind of self-observation reveals that the experience of sensory phenomena is generally a combination of external stimuli and internal perception and interpretation. The inner realm of ideas, emotions, and dreams, similarly, is seen to be a net of causal chains unfolding continuously as in the steps of dependent origination.

How much one can perceive through mindful attention depends on the care with which he observes his consciousness and the energy he devotes to self-awareness. Greater mindfulness produces deeper understanding of the nature of consciousness and broader awareness of the causal factors generating suffering for oneself and others. As the practitioner increases his mindfulness, he becomes ever more aware of his mental and physical actions, and those of others, and learns ever more about the causes of all things.

Although mindfulness is usefully directed to any aspects of human experience, including the past and the future, the near and the distant, it is most beneficial when directed to the immediate present, to the instantaneous now and here of one's own being.

Right Meditation

Buddhist meditation (dhyana) is the concentration of awareness on a focus of attention leading to pacification of the mind, understanding of consciousness, and the development of compassion. It is the concentrated application of mindfulness to the inner experience of consciousness.

To penetrate the confusions and illusions generated by sensory and mental experiences, one must become familiar with the inner mind of pure consciousness. As one becomes more familiar with the fundamental nature of consciousness, he becomes more capable of distinguishing thoughts and sensations from the underlying, innermost consciousness. Developing recognition and understanding of one's inner consciousness enables one gradually to escape the fetters and sufferings produced by self-centered misinterpretations of experience. The belief that one is a permanent self defending his identity, for example, is very hard to escape unless one directly experiences the selflessness of the inner mind.

It is the function of meditation to penetrate such illusions and allow one to observe the operations of the mind “up close” and with calm detachment from the normal flood of thoughts and feelings. Seeing the mind in calm concentration allows the meditator to gain far-reaching insight into its characteristics, especially insight into the nature of the formless, impersonal, and pervasive core of consciousness.

Although a thoughtful person can attain a conceptual understanding of emptiness through a process of reasoning, intellectual understanding alone is not sufficient to reveal the full nature of empty, primordial consciousness. Meditation allows one to experience directly the inner nature of consciousness, along with the causal processes generating thoughts and other phenomena. It was the practice of self-study through meditation that revealed to Siddhartha the elemental causes of human suffering and the means of ending it.

In traditional Sanskrit terminology, the word “dhyana” denotes the practice of meditation, and the word “samadhi” refers to the state of mind realized by the skillful meditator. There are many forms of meditation that can produce greater understanding of the inner mind. Guidance from experienced practitioners is always recommended. In general, the “right meditation” advocated by the Buddha consists of the cultivation of a stable samadhi in which the practitioner, in a state of tranquility and alertness, can observe, directly and without conceptual elaboration, both the presence and absence of thoughts, and the pure inner awareness that is continually manifest.

The most common meditation techniques in Buddhist practice involve alternating or interacting phases in which one develops mental tranquility and direct knowledge of the inner nature of mind. The meditator begins with relaxation and concentration practices, such as focusing attention on the breath or on an object or sound. By drawing the mental view away from discursive thought and concentrating it into the present moment, the meditator comes to experience both the insubstantiality of thoughts and the lasting, boundless awareness that animates the inner mind. As he lets his conscious awareness sink more deeply into the unconditioned center of pure consciousness, he finds an infinite and selfless dimension of peace and creative potential that permeates all the dharmas of human experience.

The Unity of the Dharma Path

The Buddha's Noble Eightfold Path is often symbolized by a wheel with eight spokes called the dharma wheel (dharmachakra), and the Buddha's teaching is described as turning this wheel. As the eight spokes of the dharma wheel all run from the rim of the wheel to the central hub, the eight aspects of the path unite in purpose and function. The eight parts of the path are interdependent and inseparable. They are not meant to be separate steps pursued sequentially or alternately, but mutually reinforcing tasks to be pursued simultaneously. Right understanding, right intention, right speech, right action, right livelihood, right effort, right mindfulness, and right meditation all are needed to tame the ego-driven mind, overcome the delusions of sensation, emotion, and unbalanced conceptualization, and guide the aspirant toward the skillful choices that will harvest the fruits of the inner mind and transform the surrounding world.

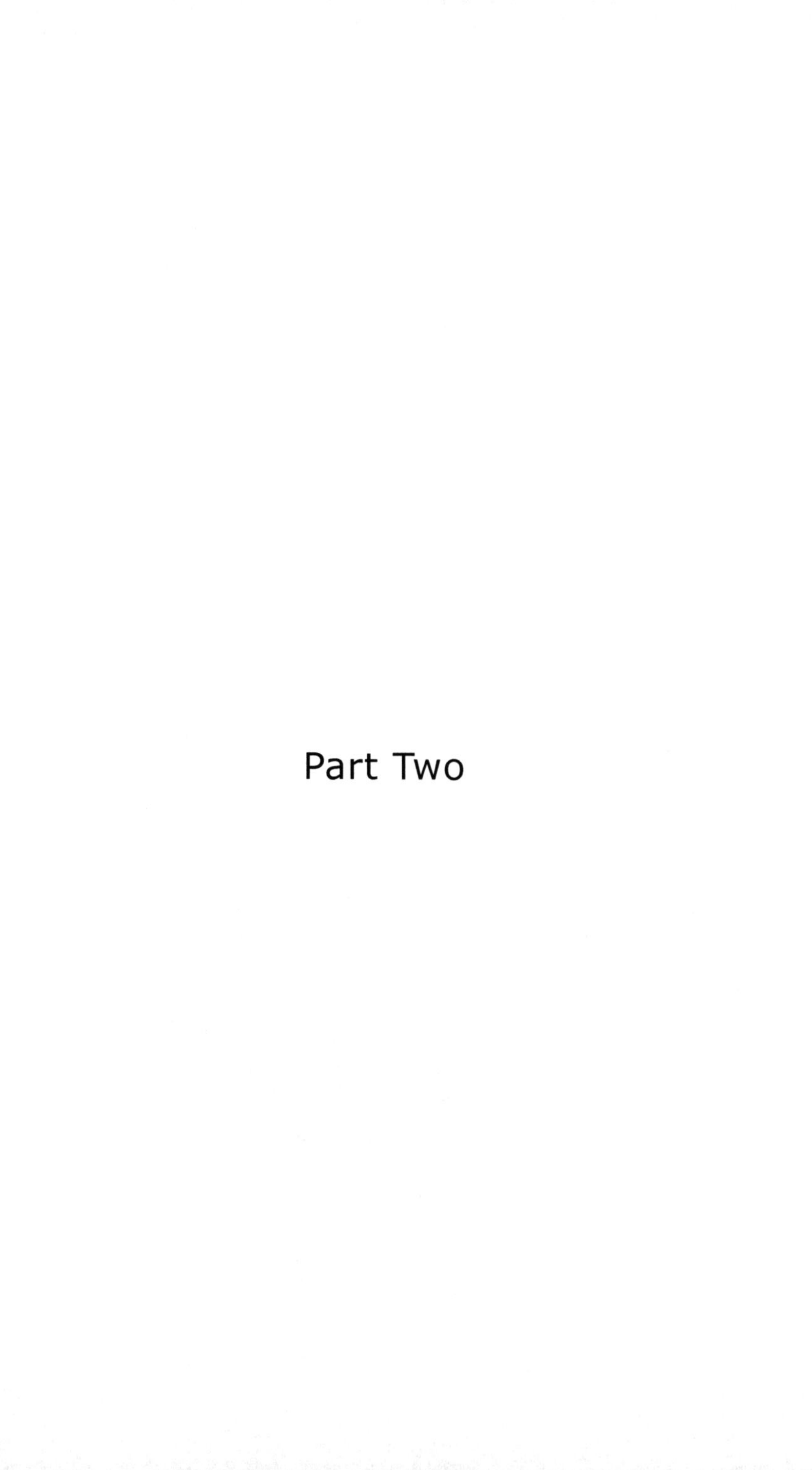

Part Two

The Second Turning of the Dharma Wheel: Universal Emptiness and the Bodhisattva Ideal

The second turning of the dharma wheel refers to a large group of further teachings on emptiness and enlightenment, often embodied in texts produced by the sangha several centuries after the death of Shakyamuni, which emphasized cultivation of an altruistic ideal rooted in the experience of selflessness. These teachings gave rise to a wide variety of philosophical schools, including some concentrating on metaphysical or psychological analysis, some concentrating on lay, non-monastic practice, and some de-emphasizing all scriptural traditions and emphasizing spontaneous insight into the nature of mind and phenomena.

Any of the earlier or later arising dharma traditions might be found in combination with others, and all had essential common elements, especially the foundation of the first turning of the teachings.

Often the later teachings were said to have been imparted selectively by the Buddha, either to particular followers or audiences, or under various admonitions of caution or secrecy.

The broader philosophical and social focuses of the later evolutions of buddhadharma led to their being characterized as part of a greater vehicle (mahayana) for the transport of beings to enlightenment, in contrast to the supposedly smaller vehicle (hinayana) of the older teachings. As buddhadharma is fundamentally a matter of personal mental experience in an infinite field of potential consciousness, all verbal characterizations of it are ultimately inadequate. Whatever sort of vehicle the practitioner may chance to try, the destination of selflessness is always beyond material or verbal conquest and also always immediately available to everyone.

In the second cycle of the Buddha's teachings the understanding of emptiness (shunyata) was expanded. While the earlier teachings had emphasized the emptiness of the self, the conscious individual, the later teachings gave similar attention to the emptiness of things, or phenomena perceived as external to the individual. Sometimes this distinction is referred to as the emptiness of self and the emptiness of other, or the selflessness of persons and the selflessness of things.

As with personal emptiness, the emptiness of phenomena can be logically deduced from the interdependence and the relativity of phenomena; from analysis of the subdivisions of space and time, and parts and wholes; from analysis of the meanings of words and concepts; and so forth. The emptiness of things can also be experienced directly, though habits of perception and interpretation present substantial obstacles to unconditional insight in this regard.

Ordinary experience, however, readily demonstrates the impermanence of virtually all things and their dependence on many causal and perceptual processes. Both experience and reasoning reveal that nothing in the physical or mental worlds has a fixed, permanent, and independent or unconditional existence. Everything is always in a state of change, moving from existence to nonexistence, depending on all the external and internal conditions affecting its appearance and the perceptions and conceptions of beings. Some dharma teachers have referred to the manifestation of emptiness as "interbeing." Nothing exists just as itself. Everything exists only as a temporary reality dependent on the momentary conditions of it and everything else. The being of anything is really always an interbeing with everything else.

The psychological and philosophical implications of dependent origination, emptiness, and interbeing are profound. Nothing is ever only as it appears to a particular point of view. What appears long to one is short to another. Right and wrong, good and bad, true and false, and all other characterizations are essentially relative and conditional. In the universe of variable perceptions and dependent ideas, all things can only be both so and not so. There is no absolute or permanent "reality," but only a shifting field of ideas and impressions, condensing here and there into various patterns of collective perception, as long recognized by rationalist thinkers of many cultures.

By embracing philosophical relativism and verbal paradox, the later followers of Shakyamuni transformed the Middle Way into a truly universal doctrine that transcended all mental categories in revealing the limitations of words and concepts and exposing the realm of pure consciousness to intellectual view.

There are indeed ideas and conditional realities that both do and do not exist at the same time. Mahayana philosophy provided intellectual and experiential tools for the analysis and understanding of the whole range of human consciousness, including both the ordinary and the more extraordinary dimensions of the mind.

In the first cycle of his teachings the Buddha emphasized the impermanence of conditioned dharmas and exhorted his followers to realize the nirvana of the unconditioned mind. The second cycle of teachings elaborated on the nature and manifestations of the unconditioned realm, the realm of transcendent, noumenal experience also designated by such terms as the Uncaused, the Uncreated, and the Unborn. The exploration of unconditional reality led practitioners to a new understanding of the phenomenal world that sees it as generated by a potent adjoining emptiness from which it emerges and into which it dissolves. This empty matrix of the apparent world is found in the bare, open consciousness of the inner mind, where, it was said, beings could find relief from misery and ultimately freedom from the bonds of birth and death.

The Bodhisattva Ideal

The goal of spiritual practice expressed in the earliest dharma teachings, the nirvana or enlightenment sought by the earliest practitioners, was usually described as the transcendence of samsaric suffering and the liberation of the individual into the unconditioned realm of peace found through the diligent pursuit of the noble eightfold path. The attainment of nirvana implied freedom from rebirth and continual experience of the bliss of selflessness and of detachment from material concerns.

The second wave of dharma teachings criticized the adepts of the earlier traditions for concentrating on their own liberation and neglecting the welfare of other persons. The exponents of the second turning created a new ideal for dharma practice. Instead of the goal of personal liberation, they promoted the goal of universal liberation, expressed in the commitment of the bodhisattva, the being committed not only to his own enlightenment, but also to the enlightenment of all other beings. The bodhisattvas were described as persons on the dharma path who chose to postpone their ultimate enlightenment (buddhahood) and removal from samsara until all other beings had first attained that state. The bodhisattvas were said to voluntarily endure rebirth in samsara in order to guide all other beings to enlightenment.

Mahayana buddhists considered the enlightenment of the bodhisattvas to be superior to that of earlier practitioners who achieved merely personal liberation, remaining detached from the sufferings of others. The bodhisattvas were said to more fully understand both the emptiness of persons and the emptiness of things. According to the mahayana teachings, unless a practitioner could commit himself to the welfare of other beings, his realization of inner selflessness must be too imperfect to constitute the full enlightenment of a buddha. For the buddhists of the second turning, to realize emptiness was to realize compassion.

The benevolent ideal of the bodhisattva dedicated to the salvation of others became ever more popular among buddhist practitioners. Meditation on emptiness and compassion gave them access to the mentality of the bodhisattvas, and contemplation of both abstract and historical examples of buddhas and bodhisattvas led pious laymen and monastics alike to emulation of the conduct of the great beings.

It became expedient to identify various transcendent bodhisattvas and buddhas as models of perfect enlightenment and to describe their unceasing action in the world as sustaining and providential. Depicted as inhabiting celestial realms from which they responded with infinite compassion and skill to the needs of the human world, these transcendent beings offered hope and inspiration to dharma practitioners, often becoming subjects of extensive devotional practices. Seen as personifications of enlightened mind and enduring symbols of the infinitely varying activity of enlightened beings in human society, the celestial bodhisattvas and buddhas became familiar elements of mahayana meditation, prayer, ritual, art, and literature. These transcendent figures included such entities as Avalokiteshvara, the Bodhisattva of Compassion; Maitreya, the Future Buddha; Manjushri, the Bodhisattva of Wisdom; Bhaisajyaguru, the Medicine Buddha; the Bodhisattvas Samantabhadra, Vajrapani, and Kshitigarbha; and many, many others.

The symbolism and dharma usages associated with the supernatural bodhisattvas and buddhas resemble some of those associated with the Three

Kayas of the Buddha and with the yidams of the third cycle of the Buddha's teachings. These doctrines and usages have many varieties, complexities, and subtleties and are best pursued under the personal guidance of highly qualified dharma teachers.

Bodhichitta: the Unity of Emptiness and Compassion

The Sanskrit word for enlightenment is "bodhi," from the same linguistic root as "buddha," one who is enlightened. A "bodhisattva" is an "enlightenment being" or a "wisdom being," one progressing toward full awakening and committed to achieving the full realization of selflessness.

The way of the bodhisattva is often summarized as a combination of wisdom and skillful means (prajna and upaya). Wisdom is right understanding of mind and phenomena, especially understanding of emptiness, personal and universal. Skillful means, which could be described as knowledge and willful actions employed in the selfless service of mankind, comprises the activities of the bodhisattvas. The bodhisattvas undertake to lead all beings to enlightenment, freeing them from the sufferings of samsara and introducing them to the pleasures of nirvana and a selfless life. Such a task requires extraordinary insight, determination, judgment, and energy, as well as other qualities and aptitudes produced only rarely in human development.

According to the teachings of the bodhisattvas, the key to the development of the bodhisattva's mind and action is called "bodhichitta." Meaning literally "the mind of enlightenment," and also translated as "enlightened attitude," "enlightening mind," and "the seed of enlightenment," bodhichitta is the mentality that comprehends emptiness, actualizes the eightfold path, and resolves to devote all its energies, life after life, to the liberation of all sentient beings from the illusions and sufferings of corporeal existence. Traditionally, bodhichitta is said to have two aspects, relative and absolute. Relative bodhichitta is usually described as the aspiration to attain enlightenment for the benefit of all sentient beings, combined with selfless action to accomplish universal enlightenment. Absolute or ultimate bodhichitta is described as the ultimate understanding of emptiness, the interdependent, unreal nature of apparent phenomena. Both aspects of bodhichitta motivate and empower the bodhisattvas to fulfill their selfless commitments. While from the relative point of view, the bodhisattvas are saving people from suffering and illusion, from the point of view of absolute emptiness, both the bodhisattvas and those they help are only momentary, conditional manifestations of the enduring, impersonal, and formless reality of emptiness.

The apparent mystery of how the realization of emptiness generates the most far-reaching love and compassion dissolves when the practitioner experiences the emptiness of the inner mind. As the great bodhisattvas have taught for centuries, the very essence of emptiness is compassion. One who realizes inner emptiness immediately realizes compassion as well. It is the natural instinct of one freed from self-centered illusion.

The dharma teachers of the second cycle have produced innumerable exercises, meditations, studies, and other practices skillfully designed to reveal and develop insight and compassion among people. Long experience has shown that the development of altruistic compassion goes hand in hand with the realization of emptiness. Each causes the other. The cultivation of compassion is so integral to the understanding of emptiness that the skillful means by which bodhisattvas lead people to enlightenment are often described simply as infinite forms of compassion. One of the best known practices for the cultivation of bodhichitta is mentally exchanging oneself with others, for example by blending mindfulness of others with one's own breathing, mentally absorbing the sufferings of others on inhalation and mentally bestowing peace and relief on them with exhalation.

The Four Immeasurables

Another classic bodhisattva practice for the cultivation of bodhichitta is a set of aspirations or prayers known as the Four Immeasurables. These are four limitless wishes that are extended to all beings in the following steps:

1. May all beings have happiness and the causes of happiness.
2. May they be free from suffering and the causes of suffering.
3. May they always have great joy, free of any suffering.
4. May they always rest in great equanimity, free of attachment or aversion to any beings or circumstances.

The Three Kayas of the Buddha

A major innovation of the second turning of the Dharma was the doctrine of the Three Kayas (or Trikaya) of the Buddha. "Kaya" means "body." The Trikaya is the teaching on the three bodies of the Buddha. After the death of Shakyamuni Buddha, his followers were naturally inclined to understand his life and his Dharma in the context of ongoing time, without the extraordinary physical presence of Shakyamuni and his personal teaching activities. Those who had followed Shakyamuni into the timeless, selfless realm of the Uncreated knew that there was an underlying, lasting reality in which all the problems and confusions of mundane life disappeared. To introduce this reality to all beings, they created the doctrine of the Three Kayas. This teaching held that, instead of only one human body, the Buddha always had at least three metaphysical bodies in which he forever participated: the Dharmakaya, the Sambhogakaya, and the Nirmanakaya.

The Dharmakaya, the "Reality Body" of the Buddha, was defined as the ultimate nature of the universe, the empty but infinitely manifest reality that generates all phenomena and experience. The Dharmakaya was said to be the ultimate mind of the Buddha, as well as the essence of all things, from the innermost mind of all beings to the infinite forms and expanses of the cosmos.

The Sambhogakaya, the "Enjoyment Body" of the Buddha, was said to be the Buddha's experience of enlightenment as well as the nature of his speech and teachings, the idea substance of his Dharma. The Sambhogakaya represents the conceptual, verbal, and communicative aspects of enlightenment. As a symbol for the lasting reality, validity, and efficacy of the dharma truths, on both the relative and the ultimate levels of conception and human action, the Sambhogakaya is actualized through the selfless activity of the enlightened ones. As dharma practitioners manifest the moral and intellectual ideals of the buddhas and the bodhisattvas, they embody the reality of the Sambhogakaya.

In Buddhist iconography the Sambhogakaya is usually depicted as an exalted buddha figure adorned with jewels and elegant silken garments.

Representing the ultimate realization of fully enlightened beings, Sambhogakaya images are also used to symbolize the Dharmakaya, especially in the third turning of the teachings.

The Nirmanakaya, the "Transformation Body" of the Buddha, is the physical body of the enlightened human being. When bodhisattvas and buddhas are said to reincarnate, the Nirmanakaya of a previous lifetime transforms into a new person of a later lifetime. In contrast, the Dharmakaya, though ultimately beyond characterization, remains eternally as it is. The Sambhogakaya, the formless, selfless manifestation of bodhichitta in the mental formations of the enlightened, though changing in conceptual content according to the circumstances and needs of the time, forever extends the saving means and insights of the Dharma to all beings through the mental and bodily actions of the Nirmanakayas. The experience and action of enlightenment can thus be an undying continuity over millennia of history.

The doctrine of the Trikaya, which has many more complexities and implications than here described, provided a useful theoretical framework for conceiving how the enduring realities of buddhist illumination could persist so thoroughly through the ages despite the continual passing away of the beings within whose minds enlightenment occurred. The concept of the Three Kayas harmonized with many other themes of the buddhadharma and stimulated much further speculation and analysis. One basic correspondence with other ideas can be seen in the parallels among the Three Jewels, the Three Kayas, and what are often called the Three Gates (Body, Speech, and Mind). The individual interacts with the world through these Three Gates of Mind, Speech, and Body. The buddhadharma is found in the Three Jewels of Buddha, Dharma, and Sangha. The Three Kayas or esoteric bodies of the Buddha which continually manifest are the Dharmakaya (the Mind of the Buddha), the Sambhogakaya (the Experience and Speech of the Buddha), and the Nirmanakaya (the Human Body of the Buddha).

Bodhichitta in Action: The Six Perfections

The philosophical outlook and the moral program of the mahayana are epitomized by the Six Perfections (paramitas). The Six Perfections are a set of virtues or qualities that define the realization of bodhichitta. They describe the mentality, the aspirations, and the activity of the bodhisattvas.

Although one cannot directly witness or evaluate the enlightenment of another person, the manifestations of bodhichitta – the inner and outer actions of enlightened mind – are always present as the Six Perfections of the bodhisattvas. The best indication of the extent to which dharma practitioners have realized the wisdom of enlightenment is the degree to which they have developed these six qualities.

The Six Perfections (paramitas) to which the bodhisattvas aspire are:

1. Generosity (danaparamita)
2. Morality (shilaparamita)
3. Patience (kshantiparamita)
4. Diligence (viryaparamita)
5. Meditation (dhyanaparamita)
6. Wisdom (prajnaparamita).

The words generosity, morality, patience, diligence, meditation, and wisdom alone do not convey the full meaning of the Six Perfections. The Sanskrit term "paramita" is crucial in signifying the meaning of these perfections. "Paramita" means "gone beyond" or "crossed over." It reflects a traditional metaphor describing the dharma path as crossing from one shore of the river of samsara to the "other shore" of nirvana. The Six Perfections have gone beyond the ordinary world to the realm of the unconditioned and the selfless. They are virtues that have gone beyond conceptualization in general, and in particular, beyond concepts of self and other, or philosophical dualism. It is the combination of emptiness or selflessness (shunyata) with the qualities ordinarily designated by these six words that reveals the actual meaning of the Six Perfections.

The Perfection of Generosity

The perfection of generosity is generosity "gone beyond" generosity. It is selfless generosity of the purest kind. To engage in truly selfless generosity, the actor must not even conceive of himself as a separately acting being. He does not think of himself as performing acts of generosity. There is no conception of pride, accomplishment, or virtue in selfless generosity. One practicing generosity with a mind wholly open to emptiness cannot fall into self-congratulation or vanity of any kind.

When emptiness is fully blended with one's actions and aspirations, it is said that one experiences threefold emptiness: emptiness of the subject, emptiness of the object, and emptiness of the action. When a gift is given in ordinary consciousness, the giver imagines that he gives a gift to another. When a gift is given in threefold emptiness, the giver conceives no giver, no recipient, and no gift. This is truly selfless giving. When the giver sees no gift, no giver, and no recipient, his act cannot be corrupted by any self-centered motivations. The act of generosity becomes a spontaneous benefit unburdened by any traces of self-interest in the actor and even unburdened by any conceptual limitations whatsoever.

As only the most enlightened persons can escape the subtlest conceptions of self and the deepest habitual patterns of perception, only rare and gifted bodhisattvas will fully realize the ideal of perfectly selfless generosity. But careful contemplation of the emptiest inner mind enables the most insightful bodhisattvas to act in the fullness of generosity beyond any conception of selfish interest. Such is the perfection of generosity, transcendent generosity gone beyond ordinary ideas about generosity.

The Perfection of Morality

The perfection of morality, often called the perfection of self-discipline, describes the morality and self-control of the bodhisattva whose mind is rooted in buddhist emptiness (shunyata). Seeing always the emptiness of all things, starting with his own selflessness, the enlightened bodhisattva is free to engage in the most skillful and beneficial conduct without the constraints of self-interested emotional and intellectual conflicts. Acting selflessly, the purest bodhisattvas are able to conform their willful actions to the highest standards of disinterested generosity and compassion. In all of their actions they seek to fulfill the aspirations of the Four Immeasurable motivations to secure the greater welfare of all beings; yet, acting from the standpoint of fundamental wisdom, they see themselves, their actions, and those they benefit as ultimately unreal and insubstantial, the passing productions of causal chains soon to dissipate in the primal, lasting reality beyond concepts.

The essence of buddhist morality is to avoid causing harm to others, joined with constant action to relieve the sufferings of others. As with all of the Six Perfections, the perspective of universal emptiness and complete selflessness adds the transcendent dimension to the virtue of moral action. Following the discipline of buddhadharma, those aspiring to the perfection of morality maintain their virtuous actions and scrupulously resist engaging in any unvirtuous actions, while striving not to conceptualize either their actions or their resistance as virtuous conduct involving ultimately existing realities. Their hearts and minds freed from self-centered ideas and feelings, and always acting with the greatest sympathy for other persons, the bodhisattvas skillfully discover the needs of beings and apply their uncommon insights and talents continually to end the causes of human suffering.

The benevolent intentions of the bodhisattvas always extend not only to all of humanity, but to all sentient beings in the universe.

The Perfection of Patience

The perfection of patience is patience beyond patience. It is patience imbued with threefold emptiness. As with the other paramitas, persons of ordinary consciousness cannot easily conceive of the perfection of patience because it is patience happening in the fullest mentality of emptiness, void of actor, action, and result. Selfless patience enables practitioners to endure the sufferings of samsara without grasping any experience as permanent or definitive. Those most aware of the empty dimensions of mind and experience see themselves, the offending stimuli, and the resulting painful experiences as empty phenomena, without inherent reality. For them the feeling self and the apparent world are always experienced as changing and passing events, like scenes in an endless, imaginary drama.

The endurance of suffering achievable by one who does not conceive suffering to be real, who does not consider himself ultimately to exist, and who does not consider endurance to be hard or painful would naturally be much greater than the endurance of which one would be capable whose mind automatically grasps as painful and agonizing the experience of suffering which he conceives to be real and which he conceives to be happening to a real and vulnerable person that is himself.

Those most familiar with the emptiness of the inner mind are not troubled by silence, stillness, or sameness, and they are able to bear tedium and boredom far more than persons unaware, or only slightly aware, of inner emptiness. The ability to overcome boredom and the loss of attention it entails is important to anyone practicing mindfulness and meditation. When, through the development of patience, the bare extension of time is no longer oppressive, and one can tolerate both frequent change in, and long continuation of, mental states, he becomes capable of experiencing the inner mind and learning directly how mental conditions arise, transform, and dissipate. For those pursuing the path to buddhist enlightenment, the ultimate philosophical goal is often verbalized as understanding the nature of mind. Without the cultivation of abundant, powerful patience, dharma practitioners would never be able to probe deeply into their own minds, and thus they would never be able to gain much understanding of their minds, nor would they be able to develop adequately the other skills and qualities necessary for the full realization of enlightenment.

The perfection of patience equips the bodhisattvas to actualize both wisdom and enlightened action in the difficult drudgery of the material world. Great patience allows them to endure the hardships of life and to accept the conditional realities of the terrestrial world precisely as they are. The bodhisattvas do not need to construct soothing imaginary worlds with which to delude themselves in order to make life on Earth bearable. Living in the universal realm of the uncreated as well as in the shifting, mostly painful whirl of samsara, they gain mental freedom from any conditions, negative or positive, imposed on them by birth-and-death.

Thus able to endure suffering and difficulty far more than ordinary persons, the enlightened bodhisattvas enjoy an immensely greater sphere of compassionate action and a much greater potential for happiness, fulfillment, and contentment in both the relative world of ordinary experience and the "other world" of selfless peace.

The Perfection of Diligence

The perfection of diligence, viryaparamita, is the perfection of effort, exertion, energy, perseverance, and willpower. The Sanskrit term connotes enthusiasm and vigor as well as exertion and continuous striving. It includes the quality of determination that enables the bodhisattvas to accomplish the impossible. The perfection of diligence joins constant effort to constant intention in the selflessness of bodhichitta.

Being selfless in all respects, transcendent diligence does not produce proud ideas of strength, persistence, determination, or heroism in the actors. What it produces is endless action and endless effort. This perfect effort is effort beyond effort, effort that never subsides, effort that never gives up or abandons its purpose. Ideally it becomes effortless effort. The bodhisattvas endowed with it appear capable of infinite exertion without ever tiring or becoming discouraged when their efforts to help beings or to overcome personal failings are unsuccessful.

There is selfless diligence in the practice of all the paramitas. It is the energy of bodhichitta – the energy and the action of the bodhisattvas. The bodhisattvas are able to accomplish so much because of their insight into primordial emptiness, because of the power of their vast intentions, and because of the relentlessness of their exertions.

The diligence of the bodhisattvas overcomes whatever obstacles may arise to frustrate their activities. It is the antidote to laziness and any deficiencies in motivation practitioners may encounter. Adopting the discipline and the goals of the bodhisattvas requires those on the dharma path to make effective judgments and choices continually, and to exert themselves energetically in all of their important endeavors. They must develop both insight and willpower in order to be able to know where, when, and how to act for the greatest benefit of others, and then to consistently do so. The bodhisattvas are not deterred by impediments, difficulties, or failures. With ongoing selfless diligence they cultivate the necessary insight and vigor, and devote unrelenting effort to relieving the material, mental, and emotional needs of all persons and helping them to discover the bountiful inner nature of the human mind.

The Perfection of Meditation

Meditation is the preeminent buddhist method of gaining understanding of consciousness and the dynamics of the inner mind. It is the practice of meditation, the calm observation of consciousness, that allows one to experience the nonconceptual, pervasive reality that is traditionally described as emptiness (shunyata). The comprehension of inner and outer emptiness, with all that it entails in freeing the mind from preconceptions and ego-generated illusions, empowers the bodhisattvas to generate the six perfections and to fulfill their vows to secure the enlightenment of all beings.

The meditation of the bodhisattvas is the accomplishment of the right effort, right mindfulness, and right meditation of the earlier teachings enhanced with the boundless motivation and energy of bodhichitta.

The various forms of meditation offering insight into the inner mind generally commence with the development of tranquility and concentration. In order to experience the essential center of consciousness, one must be able to settle through the the illusional conceptuality of the skandhas, the normal activity of the mind, and become familiar with bare consciousness, the knowing awareness of the mind unobscured by emotions, perceptions, and words. The bare awareness of the mind is found only in the present moment; therefore, meditation practice must develop one-pointedness in which the mind rests continually in the present, without drifting into conceptual thinking, memory, and anticipation.

Resting in nowness is like sitting on the threshold of an open door consisting of pure awareness. Ultimately one does not seek to analyze or conceptualize what is happening, but only to witness directly what is happening, for example, how awareness operates and gives rise to thoughts and experience. One should meditate with no thought of attainment or personal accomplishment, but only with the impulse to experience inner awareness as it naturally occurs.

Meditation can be done in both stillness and action. The bodhisattvas strive to make it a continuous state of mind, in which one is always mentally open to recognition of the processes of awareness and conceptualization that construct our phenomenal experiences. The perfection of meditation extends the practices of self-observation and inner mindfulness to all the actions and conditions of the person. With transcendent vigor and alertness, the bodhisattvas persist always in a lifelong effort to expand their understanding of the fundamental awareness that is the essence of consciousness. As the insight of practitioners increases, the boundary between meditation and non-meditation tends to disappear, and those on the bodhi path develop ever greater powers of self-awareness and understanding.

While cultivation of insight into the nature of mind is the main focus of meditation in the mahayana, many meditational practices are also designed for the development of compassion and active sympathy for other beings. During meditation sessions and in the course of daily activities bodhisattvas often exchange themselves mentally with other persons and direct their inner attentions to the needs of others. Realizing the inseparability of emptiness and compassion, the bodhisattvas naturally embody universal love and kindness as they deepen their understanding of emptiness.

It is often said that the perfections of generosity, morality, patience, diligence, and meditation constitute the skillful means (upaya) by which the bodhisattvas attain wisdom or understanding (prajna), as well as the means by which the bodhisattvas accomplish their commitments in the light of their growing understanding. The first five perfections are thus distinguished from the sixth, categorizing the paramitas into two groups corresponding respectively to the means and wisdom aspects of the path, both aspects of which are always interdependent and mutually active in generating human enlightenment. The perfection of meditation is the engine of all the others. By means of skillful and energetic meditation, the bodhisattvas cultivate realization of both the conditional and the ultimate aspects of enlightened mind, eventually actualizing the qualities and activities of the buddhas.

The Perfection of Wisdom

The perfection of wisdom, prajnaparamita, is ultimate understanding of the nature of mind and phenomena. It is the wisdom that comprehends emptiness and establishes the philosophical foundation of mahayana buddhism. It is the core insight of bodhichitta, the mentality of the bodhisattvas, that which generates enlightenment. It is the insight that animates all of the Six Perfections and elevates them to the realm of inconceivability.

Understanding that mind and phenomena are ultimately "empty" does not enable one to describe that emptiness in words or to conceive of it in exact ideas. The empty nature of mind and its perceptions can be experienced, but it cannot be defined. It is too vast and complex in all of its manifestations, while also having an infinite and inexpressible simplicity and continuity. It is forever changing and forever the same. It could be called both nothing and everything. It has been called a middle way between existence and nonexistence.

Since no idea or statement can express all of the characteristics of the mind (or the phenomena it experiences), buddhist teachers often deny whatever is asserted about it. An ancient formulation maintains that it cannot be said of mind: (1) that it exists, (2) that it does not exist, (3) that it both exists and does not exist, or (4) that it neither exists nor does not exist.

The paradoxical nature of mind and reality that is known through perfect wisdom has traditionally been indicated by terms like emptiness, suchness, interbeing, and dharmakaya. Eluding expression and conceptualization, this underlying reality is experienced and recognized through the cultivation of wisdom.

The totality of mental and material phenomena that appear to sentient beings constitutes conditioned existence, or samsara. The enlightenment of the buddhas is said to be a coexisting but radically different state of mind in which one experiences the inner realm of the mind as a peaceful, unconditional, and unchanging reality, called nirvana, continuing undiminished through all of the changing experiences of samsara.

The divergent experiences of samsara and nirvana are often condensed into the terms "form" and "emptiness." "Form" represents the changing, apparent world of the senses and the thinking mind. "Emptiness" represents the unchanging, permanent reality in which samsaric appearances arise and fade. The perfection of wisdom sees that emptiness and form are two aspects of one universal reality. The wisdom teachings of the bodhisattvas express this understanding by stating that form is emptiness, and emptiness is form.

Understanding that neither the thinking self nor the world it appears to experience has any independent reality, the bodhisattvas who accomplish the perfection of wisdom experience samsara and nirvana as one and the same. The insight that reveals the emptiness of the phenomenal world reveals the emptiness of nirvana as well. The wisdom realized by the bodhisattvas knows emptiness to be the nature of all things: mind and matter, bondage and liberation, suffering and peace. This universal, indescribable reality verbally symbolized as the cosmic mind of the Buddha (the Dharmakaya) is beyond conceptual determination, yet it manifests as enlightenment, the activities of the buddhas, and all the appearances of the phenomenal world.

Understanding emptiness is integral to all buddhist practice. To encounter selflessness and interdependence is to encounter compassion and karma, the wellsprings of buddhist morality, judgment, and motivation. All of the skillful means by which buddhas and bodhisattvas lead people to peace and enlightenment are crucially informed by the wisdom that grasps the reality of emptiness. A traditional epithet for the perfection of wisdom is "the Mother of All the Buddhas."

As understanding emptiness is understanding the nature of mind and existence, there are infinitely many ways it may occur to individuals. The perfection of this understanding expresses the threefold emptiness that characterizes the other transcendent perfections of the bodhisattvas.

Being beyond conceptualization and devoid of dualistic perception, the perfection of wisdom never identifies a knower of this wisdom, a truth that can be known, or an act of knowledge. Ultimately the inexpressible nature of all things that is called "emptiness" for convenience can only be known authentically through a nonconceptual, personal realization in the inner core of conscious awareness.

Studying, contemplating, and realizing the nature of mind is the essence of the buddhist path. Over the centuries since Shakyamuni perfected this realization and communicated its providential wisdom to his contemporaries, his successors have practiced many different means of cultivating this essential understanding. In what is known as the third cycle of of the Buddha's teachings, powerful new methods were added to the wisdom tradition. Regardless of the means pursued by different practitioners, the goal of all buddhadharma has continued to be the liberation of beings from the self-imposed conceptual and emotional delusions condemning them to the bewildering miseries of mistaking their passing mental experiences for lasting truths.

As an illustration of this constant goal, the Appendix to this Summary contains a form of the Bodhisattva Vow, by which many buddhists continue to commit themselves to the selfless purposes of the bodhisattvas. Also included in the Appendix are two brief verses that epitomize the wisdom of the bodhisattvas: a modern composition of Soen Nakagawa Roshi and the concluding admonition of the Buddha from the Diamond Sutra, a classical mahayana exposition on the perfection of wisdom.

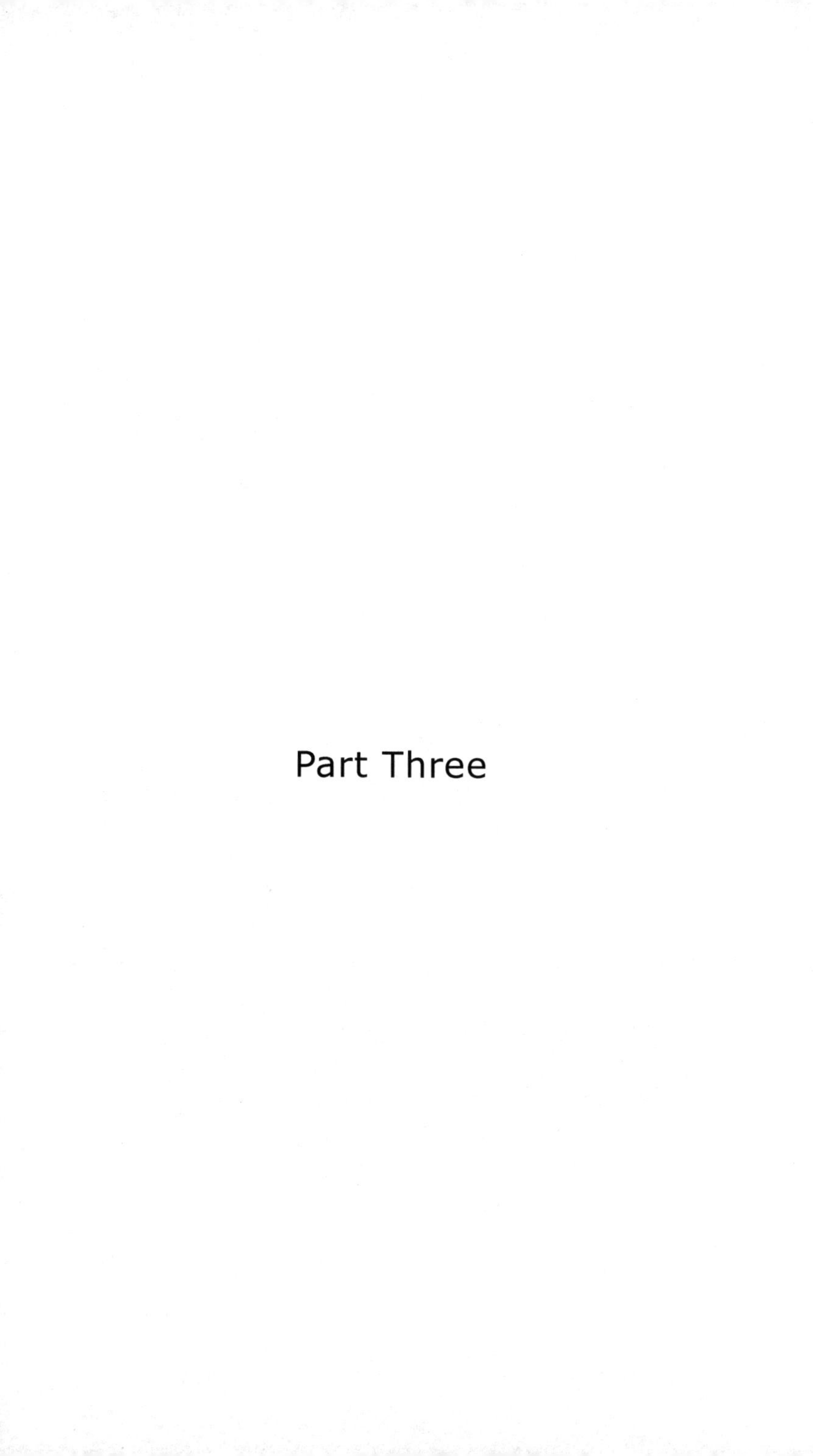

Part Three

The Third Turning of the Dharma Wheel: Buddha Nature and Immanent Wisdom

The insights of the mahayana practitioners opened a vast field of self-development to individualized and institutional cultivation by followers of the buddhist path. The pursuit of wisdom through meditation and self-awareness could be combined with many different kinds of spiritual practices and lifestyles, according to personal inclinations and circumstances. Understanding the nature of mind and phenomena could be cultivated by anyone, at any moment.

Buddha Nature

The third cycle of dharma teachings emphasized immediate experience of the full nature of reality. This full nature, the infinite, interdependent realm of emptiness and phenomenal appearances, was called Buddha Nature. As an abstraction representing the essence of all consciousness and experience, Buddha Nature is ultimately beyond concept or definition, but its action and manifestations are ubiquitous and continuous. It is the impersonal awareness active in all beings that experiences the phenomena of samsara and nirvana: the sensory world, the mental world, and all the nameless insights that encounter the underlying unity of all things. It is the boundless inner nature known to the enlightened ones and said by them to be the beginning and the end of the buddhist path.

Starting directly from the essential inner reality, the teachings of the third turning expanded those of the first and second turnings by elaborating on the characteristics of the universal inner nature. While reaffirming what had been called the emptiness of persons and things, the teachings on Buddha Nature called attention to the knowing, perceptual quality of pure consciousness, and to the stable mental characteristics caused by awareness of this inner reality. The classical teachings on emptiness revealed the ephemeral insubstantiality of the dharmas of consciousness. The teachings on Buddha Nature revealed what was lasting in the experiences of consciousness.

Concentrating on the fundamental nature of mind, third turning practitioners were reminded that the awakened state of the buddhas, the goal of their spiritual efforts, was awakening to the original, natural condition of all beings. What was necessary for the selfless wisdom and compassionate action of the enlightened ones to appear was elimination of the conceptual and emotional delusions that came to conceal the innermost nature in the course of human life. Removing the obscurations generated by ignorance of the fundamental nature revealed that the fully enlightened mind was always present as the underlying reality even when its nature was not recognized.

Those who sought to realize the selfless wisdom of the inner mind did not need to suppress their ordinary thinking or replace it with new ideas. They could penetrate the illusions of self-centered consciousness by direct experience of the inner awareness in the midst of ordinary sensations and mental activity. Even within a mistaken or harmful thought, the inner light of Buddha Nature still shone exactly as it did within the most exalted thoughts, and just as it did when thoughts were silenced in the stillness of meditation.

The reality referred to as Buddha Nature had many synonyms in dharma teaching. Sometimes it was called the nature of truth, or basic goodness, or the womb of the buddhas. The idea served to illuminate the nature of enlightenment and to suggest, in both theory and practice, how such a transformation of consciousness could occur.

Understanding selfless awareness to be the essence of consciousness, the primordial condition of all sentient beings, gave a convincing explanation for its full manifestation in exceptional individuals and potentially in all persons. Analysis of the psychological conditions producing illusions of independent souls and fixed external realities led to greater understanding of how the pure original nature could be obscured by growing conceptual confusion. Practical experience with diverse techniques of meditation and mental training revealed readily available means to counter such egoistic illusions and bring forth the powerful qualities described as bodhichitta and the benevolent activities of the bodhisattvas.

The importance of Buddha Nature in the third dharma cycle illustrates one of the main themes of this new wave of practice and instruction: the immanence of enlightenment, transcendent wisdom, or buddhahood, right here and now, in the ordinary experiences of daily life. The overriding message of the third turning was that ordinary mind is Buddha Nature, and that this ultimate truth could be realized and experienced by anyone, in this very body, in this very life.

Before understanding the full nature of his mind, the practitioner could conceive of it as the latent potentiality for enlightenment. After realizing the ultimate inner nature, he would know his mind to be the Dharmakaya, the one and only eternal reality, finally revealed as the essence of all things.

Another distinctive aspect of the third turning was the use of various meditation techniques commonly involving energetic imagination and yogic discipline, by which practitioners enhanced and expedited their understanding of emptiness, Buddha Nature, and phenomenal appearances. These techniques often involved mental visualization and recitation of mantras; and they were well adapted for engagement of any of the sensory or mental faculties in the generation of profound understanding and compassion. Some of the third-turning meditation practices involved manipulation of bodily energies, control of physiological processes, and other unusual forms of mental and physical self-control.

The visualization of imaginative forms and beings such as mandalas and yidams (meditational deities) afforded insights into the emptiness of visual and tactile impressions and associated self concepts. The skillful use of sound and the aural abstractions of mantra tended to reveal the empty relativities of speech and thought, and to channel consciousness deeper into the realm of nonconceptual awareness. Practices as different as ascetic yoga and the mindful experience of sensory pleasure could lead equally to the transcendence of self and the discovery of inner truth. Focusing always on the essential inner experiences of consciousness in the course of any phenomena, practitioners of these methods gained greater understanding of the fundamental, persistent qualities of ultimate reality.

The teachings of Shakyamuni Buddha, originally expressed in oral transmissions, were later compiled into a body of scriptural writings called sutras. The first and second cycles of dharma teachings both formed part of the broad sutra tradition, and the teachings on Buddha Nature were also presented in some of the sutras. Another body of writings that emerged in the centuries after Shakyamuni consisted of ritual texts and meditation guides called tantras which described some of the meditation practices developed in the third turning of buddhist teachings. Practice traditions grounded in the tantras emerged parallel to those of the sutras. These tantric traditions came to embody for many the mainstream of the third turning, and the third-cycle teachings are sometimes called "tantric buddhism." This description is incomplete since the third turning finds expression in both the sutra and the tantra literature, as well as in consummate oral and written teachings that transcend and unify all of the separate practice traditions.

The diverse teachings of the third turning are natural evolutions from those of the first and second turnings and are essentially implied in the earlier teachings. Their compassionate aim, the enlightenment of all beings, is no different from the aspiration of all the bodhisattvas. Although the ultimate nature of selfless wisdom, the supreme realization of the enlightened ones, is a universal reality knowing no distinctions based on the different paths by which it may be reached, the means used to produce and sustain the highest insight by direct awareness of the inner nature were so distinctive that they came to be identified as a third vehicle of progress toward realization. Supplementing the "hinayana" and the "mahayana," the so-called smaller and larger dharma vehicles, the third-cycle teachings came to be known as the "vajrayana" or the indestructible vehicle. Vajra was an indestructible substance of Indian mythology identified with a divine scepter, with thunderbolts, and with unassailable truth and power. The vajrayana path was often described as the diamond or adamantine path. It was said to be a quicker, more effective way to attain the insights of the bodhisattvas and to realize the perfection of selfless wisdom.

Because of the salience of mantra meditation in third turning practices, the vajrayana is also referred to as the "mantrayana" or the vehicle of secret mantra.

Contemporary vajrayana teachers have summarized the three turnings by saying that the hinayana emphasizes the abandonment of mental faults and illusions; the mahayana emphasizes the transformation of delusions into wisdom; and the vajrayana emphasizes the immediate recognition of the inner nature of both delusion and wisdom to be a single, pure, and indestructible awareness.

The three dharma vehicles that emerged from the three turnings of buddhist doctrine were complementary aspects of a broad wisdom tradition that was essentially united on the main points of philosophy, ethics, and practice. The goal of ending human suffering through the awakening of inner awareness was shared by all schools. Understanding the true nature of mind was the wisdom (prajna) sought by all buddhists, but the development of different schools showed that there were many different kinds of skillful means (upaya) by which understanding could be gained and taught.

The creative methods developed in the vajrayana expanded the range of tools available to dharma practitioners as well as their opportunities for meditation and constructive introspection; but for all its novelties, the vajrayana rests solidly on the foundations of the hinayana and the mahayana. It is important to emphasize that the dramatic techniques of the vajrayana can only be effective for those who have already internalized the aspirations of bodhichitta, the Six Perfections, and the basic view of the mahayana and hinayana teachings.

Experiencing Buddha Nature

As the inner nature of consciousness, Buddha Nature can be experienced by anyone through meditation and other forms of self-awareness. But as a sense organ cannot perceive itself, the self-reflecting mind can never comprehend the whole reality of its existence. Furthermore, according to the usual mahayana view, the mind, like all concepts and perceptions, is actually empty of any absolute and independent reality at all. Ultimately it is beyond the conceptual categories of existence and non-existence. The full nature of mind is a mystery only relatively and conditionally subject to human understanding. When buddhist practitioners seek to understand the nature of mind, they do so from the point of view of threefold emptiness and resist ascribing ultimate reality to their ideas and observations.

As subtle and paradoxical as the nature of mind appears to be from the perspective of ordinary conceptual consciousness, it can be fruitfully investigated with the skillful methods of the Middle Way, especially by persons motivated by bodhichitta and willing to engage in the direct experience of the pure inner mind without the limiting and misleading overlays of discursive thought and mental analysis. From the earliest teachings of Shakyamuni through all the benevolent articulations of his successors, the buddhadharma has prompted people of every possible sort to confront the inner mysteries of consciousness with the means at their disposal and to find the peace and satisfaction lying within the turbulent transformations always shifting back and forth between birth and death, nothingness and conditional existence.

Those who have directly studied the unconditional, changeless nature appearing to exist permanently in the midst of constant mental and phenomenal change declare that, even though it cannot really be described in words, it can be known and recognized, and certain of its apparent qualities generally identified. According to the bodhisattvas of the vajrayana, this universal inner reality is always empty, transparent to mental awareness, and infinite in the productivity and variety of its manifestations. These three characteristics of Buddha Nature are often referred to as emptiness, clarity (or luminosity), and infinite manifestation.

The emptiness of Buddha Nature is the emptiness (shunyata) of ultimate bodhichitta, the experience of the mind as having no fixed reality or inherent characteristics. Pure consciousness reveals itself in meditation to have absolutely no fixed content. It is a totally blank state of potentiality, often likened to the void of empty space.

The clarity or luminosity of Buddha Nature is the state of awareness that is always present in waking consciousness, as well as in some dream states. The inner mind is not just an empty field. When awake and alert it is constantly aware of what it experiences. This awareness is the essential experience of all thought and subjective mental phenomena. In buddhist teachings mental awareness is often described by the metaphor of light or illumination, but this is not meant literally as a visual phenomenon. When the mind is described as luminous emptiness, this usually refers to the knowing, aware nature of the mental emptiness, and not necessarily to a literal shining of light in the inner space.

The infinite manifestation of Buddha Nature refers to all phenomena that appear to the mind. This quality of mind is often described as unobstructedness or unimpededness. It is simply the conceptual universe of all appearances that arise within the mind. As long as there is consciousness it manifests endlessly in all the experiences of samsara and nirvana. No matter how confused or enlightened a mind may be, it continually experiences the thoughts, feelings, images, and other sensations generated incessantly by the forces of consciousness, just as originally demonstrated by Shakyamuni Buddha in his twelve links of dependent origination.

Analyzing the causal sequences of mental experience in the context of direct awareness of the fundamental nature of consciousness, third-cycle dharma practitioners expanded conventional understanding of the nature of enlightenment. To the traditional presentations in terms of the body, speech, and mind of the buddhas, they added teachings on the qualities and activities of the buddhas. The qualities and activities of enlightened beings were not different from those so richly described in the past, but the teachings of the third turning emphasized that the virtues and benevolent conduct of the buddhas and bodhisattvas were spontaneously present as natural aspects of their being. Perfect wisdom, compassion, and saving action were the spontaneous fruit of fully realizing the actual inner nature of all beings.

The Three Roots

The practices of the vajrayana added several new focuses to the traditional emphasis on the Three Jewels of the Buddha, the Dharma, and the Sangha. The Three Jewels remain the principal "objects of refuge" for all practitioners on the buddhist path, but the third cycle of teachings added three additional sources of refuge for those eager to escape the confusions and sufferings of material existence. These three, which came to be known as the Three Roots, are the Guru, the Yidam, and the Dharma Protectors.

The Guru is the personal teacher, guide, or spiritual friend who introduces the practitioner to the true nature of mind and guides him on the path to enlightenment. The role of the Guru is central in third-cycle teachings, many of which are imparted only by personal transmission. In the vajrayana the Guru is called the root of blessings.

All schools of buddhism recognize the importance of spiritual masters, practitioners of advanced wisdom and skill, in the propagation of buddhadharma. The nature of bodhichitta, the deep understanding of the emptiness, compassion, and insight found at the heart of consciousness, is such that it can be generated and enhanced by contact with persons who have already attained great realization of these qualities. The reverence accorded to the great bodhisattvas reflects their importance in actualizing and sustaining the Dharma and the Sangha, the spiritual community. Masterful gurus serve as teachers, advisers, holders of the dharma traditions, and as models and examples of enlightened behavior. Ultimately the eminence of the spiritual masters expresses the essential truth that enlightenment is not merely an idea or a doctrine, but an experience lived by a human being in the immanent reality of the conscious mind. Fundamentally, enlightenment is the living experience of enlightened beings. It is the experience of the buddhas as their personal awareness encounters the unconditioned realm of infinite being in the formless field of the inner mind.

The vajrayana gives special emphasis to the spiritual guide, teaching that the more the student develops faith and devotion toward his guru, the more effective the guru's actions become in awakening the wisdom and compassion of the student. The flowering of enlightenment is often directly stimulated by a person-to-person transmission of understanding, with or without words, from the guru to those he teaches. The guru can virtually replicate the action of the buddhas in awakening the primordial insight at the core of consciousness among those with whom he interacts. The guru conveys spiritual power not only by virtue of his own insight and commitments, but also because of the historical traditions with which he is associated. Many buddhist schools and lineages have long histories in which spiritual insight has been communicated person-to-person for many generations.

The essential qualities of the dharmakaya are eternal and changeless throughout time and space. When the minds of student and guru meet, it is a repetition of a universal act of recognition in which the mind becomes aware of its own enduring nature as well as the ultimate nature of the universe, as it can be known through the medium of human consciousness.

Yidams, often called meditational deities, are imaginary beings visualized in many forms of vajrayana meditation in order to generate greater insight into the nature of mind and phenomenal appearances, and to provide further means of self-strengthening for those on the bodhi path. Yidams are potent, multifaceted symbols capable of expressing the essential truths and practices of buddhadharma in highly concentrated images and mental actions. They personify mind, consciousness, and the ultimate nature of reality. They represent all of the kayas of enlightenment: the dharmakaya, the sambhogakaya, and the nirmanakaya. In short, they are symbols of buddha nature in all its manifestations.

As symbols of the dharmakaya, yidams such as Samantabhadra and Vajradhara are called primordial buddhas. These and other yidams are often seen as representations of the guru and his activity. A primordial buddha yidam may represent in one humanistic symbol the entire history of buddhadharma and the mind-to-mind transmission of insight over great periods of time.

Yidams are called the root of accomplishment, in recognition of their power to draw the practitioner toward realization and the full accomplishment of the eightfold path and the six bodhisattva perfections. One of the principal means by which yidam practice achieves these results is through the process of identification, in which the practitioner, having vividly imagined all of the characteristics of the yidam deity, including its luminous immateriality, identifies himself, his guru, or all beings as the very essence and manifestation of the yidam.

Yidams may have widely varying forms depending on their meditational functions. They may appear in peaceful, wrathful, or semi-wrathful forms, male or female forms, human or non-human forms. Gurus generally assist vajrayana students in the selection and use of yidams suitable for their personal needs and aptitudes. Yidam practice usually requires the personal instruction and guidance of qualified vajrayana teachers.

The third of the Three Roots of the vajrayana is the Dharma Protectors, often designated by the Sanskrit terms "dakas, dakinis, and dharmapalas." Dharma Protectors, like yidams, are symbolical beings reflecting an esoteric interpretation of mind and the material world. Dakas and dakinis are respectively male and female supernatural beings who stimulate enlightenment and spiritual progress in conscientious practitioners. Dharmapalas are similar beings who function to protect the Dharma teachings and remove obstacles to their propagation and realization. Referred to collectively as Dharma Protectors, these entities are known as the root of enlightened activity.

As yidams may symbolize many kinds of human and cosmic action, dharma protectors too represent a great variety of activity and experience. In general, the activity of the dharma protectors represents the benevolent action of wisdom, compassion, and buddhadharma in the human world. Spiritual friends and helpers who serve in any respect to aid, guide, comfort, or inspire buddhist practitioners may be seen as supernatural spirits having the nature of dharma protectors and being constantly available with timely assistance to those in need. The role of the dharma protectors in third-cycle buddhist teachings, like that of protecting saints, spirits, and deities in other spiritual traditions, reflects the universal reality that mental imagination and conceptualization condition and transform the world of human experience.

Tantric Methods

The systems of training and meditation developed in the third cycle of the Buddha's teaching encompassed many kinds of practice and discipline. Creative imagination and intensive forms of concentration were often used to bring the practitioner's attention to bear on the inner dimensions of mental and physical experience. Meditational practices – including recitation of mantras and tantric texts; visualization of yidams, mandalas, and other images; use of bells, horns, drums, and ritual implements; prostrations, offerings, and other kinds of symbolic gestures and actions – were used with persistent exertion of mental focus to expose to the practitioner the constant inner core of his ever-changing mentality.

This inner core of consciousness, though accessible to contemplation and experience, cannot be known as it actually is through words or conceptual interpretations. The deep inner nature revealed through contemplative insight is always empty of conceptual content even as it generates all the qualities of self-awareness, including the discursive conceptualizing of ordinary thought and sensation. Tantric practices proved effective in exposing practitioners to the fundamental inner awareness always present as the formless and impersonal projector of conscious life.

Tantric meditation practices commonly require an initiation ritual called an empowerment in which a student is introduced to a practice, instructed in its performance, and authorized to do it. The personal transmission of tantric practices from guru to practitioner is characteristic of the vajrayana. In some rituals the guru directly demonstrates the nature of the inner mind. Often initiation into tantric practices requires the initiate to make certain commitments to the guru. Practitioners may be bound by solemn vows to maintain virtuous behavior and to perform various practices with unfailing regularity.

Because of the subtlety of the tantric teachings, the prerequisites of understanding, motivation, and transmission generally necessary for tantric instruction, and the personal relationships and commitments traditionally involved, esoteric tantric teachings are usually imparted in detail only to those personally initiated into the practices by qualified teachers. General explanations and guidance concerning the more common and elementary tantric meditation practices, however, are publicly taught and widely available.

Mantra

A meditational practice used in buddhism from the beginning but especially prevalent in the vajrayana is mantra. In mantra, combinations of words, syllables, or sounds, derived from ancient Indian languages, are repeated orally or mentally in the form of an abstract chant, in order to increase understanding of the inner mind and produce insight into the nature of sound, speech, and thought. Mantras are used in many tantric meditation practices. Vajrayana practitioners also often recite mantras in the course of ordinary daily activities.

A mantra commonly used in both ways is OM MANI PADME HUM, said to be the mantra of the Bodhisattva Avalokiteshvara. Another familiar mantra is the sequence of syllables OM AH HUM. Combined with mindful focus on the present action of the inner mind, or on the breath or other bodily rhythms, the repetitive chanting of such mantras was found to increase awareness of the inner realities of body, speech, and mind.

Mantras support and protect meditation by guiding the attention of the meditator and steering it away from distracting and misleading thoughts and perceptions. Mantric words may have discursive meaning as well as abstract significance. Thus the words MANI PADME of the mantra of Avalokiteshvara signify "the Jewel in the Lotus," a traditional buddhist metaphor for the coexistence of nirvana and samsara.

Using sound, words, and the human voice in mantra to reveal the inner features of consciousness epitomizes the vajrayana practice of engaging all of the bodily and mental capacities of the human being in the cultivation of enlightenment. Sound and the vocal and aural faculties of the human body and brain are fundamental wellsprings of language, music, and human ideation and emotion. In the vajrayana they became means for the realization of buddha nature.

Creation and Completion

One of the central practices of the vajrayana is the pattern of meditation known as creation and completion. In this practice intensive visualization of yidams, buddhas, or other representations of enlightened mind is followed by dissolution of the visualizations into the emptiness of inner awareness. The meditation usually follows a ritual text beginning with a preliminary orientation of the meditator and generation of the benevolent aspiration of bodhichitta. Then, in the creation phase, the meditator creates a vivid mental image of the yidam deity and imagines it to possess the qualities of enlightened consciousness and to exhibit the appearance and the spiritual activity identified with the envisioned being.

The yidam is seen and understood as brilliant, powerful, and having the nature of enlightened awareness. It is also seen and known as insubstantial, like a hologram made of light, and having, as all things, the ultimate nature of emptiness. After the yidam has been mentally created, the meditator may contemplate it, supplicate it, or identify himself with it, according to the textual ritual.

After a period of meditation using the visualized image, the meditator terminates the visualization and enters the completion phase of the practice. The visualization dissolves into the pure, nonconceptual awareness from which it arose, and the meditator rests in the samadhi of the inner mind. Ultimately the completion phase becomes the full realization of buddha nature, the enlightened wisdom of the most accomplished bodhisattvas.

Finishing a meditation cycle of creation and completion, the practitioner dedicates the karmic merit of his meditation toward the eventual enlightenment of all beings.

Mantra recitation is often an element of yidam meditation practice. Mantra can enhance the imaginative process of creating the yidam, and it also acts directly to draw the mind into immediate awareness of the inner reality uniting yidam, meditator, and the surrounding world. Meditation practices involving the visualization of yidams and the chanting of mantras were found to stimulate profound realizations concerning the universal inner nature.

A powerful interpretation of the practices of creation and completion is that one's body and all appearances of form should be thought of as the form of the yidam, that one's speech and all sound should be thought of as the mantra of the yidam, and that one's mind and all mental phenomena should be thought of as the samadhi of the yidam. All aspects of experience are seen as appearance-emptiness and open to the pure perception of the inner mind. Seeing apparent phenomena as the form, mantra, and samadhi of the yidam and knowing it all to be mental conception without intrinsic reality leads practitioners of tantric deity meditation to ever greater understanding of the impersonal, enduring, and infinite essence of conscious life.

Mandala

Another major element of tantric dharma practice is the concept of mandala. Mandala is a multifaceted relational concept in which spatial and geometrical relationships are used to enhance understanding of mind and the phenomenal world. A mandala is a means of representing the relationship between one's own mind and the surrounding world. The mandala, in general, is a geometrical pattern consisting of a center and a circular circumference that can be used to organize and envision many kinds of experiences. In deity meditation, the yidams are often visualized as a group of figures arranged symmetrically around a central point occupied by the meditator or a central yidam. The tantric deities are usually conceived of as belonging to an interrelated group or family of deities positioned directionally within a mandala and representing altogether an integrated and comprehensive symbol of the psychic world.

The mandala concept is often used to represent the universe. The entire universe may be imagined as a symbolic circular pattern of continents or worlds. In some tantric practices the meditator makes offerings to the guru or the enlightened beings in the form of a pattern of physical or mental symbols representing the universe, which is called a mandala offering.

A fundamental aspect of the vajrayana is the point of view that sees the inner continuity within the endlessly changing appearances of samsara – the celebrated jewel in the lotus of life. This is often described as the idea of "sacred world." The entire universe of mental and physical experience is considered fundamentally sacred as the manifestation of the dharmakaya, the nameless, transcendent reality that generates all things, most importantly the universal inner awareness that blossoms into the enlightened consciousness of the buddhas. The very world that dooms all persons to suffering, unhappiness, and death also provides the unending inner resource that makes all deliverance possible. Samsara and nirvana are always equally and inseparably available in the luminous expanse of buddha nature.

Understanding the three bodies of the buddha to be the inner nature of the universe imparts a sacred dimension to the ordinary world. With this understanding, the pious vajrayana practitioner sees all persons as essentially buddhas and all experiences as reflections and projections of the unifying inner truth. Wherever an individual is physically and mentally, he is at the center of a surrounding environment that is filled with enormous power and potentiality at every point. He inhabits an infinity of mandalas open to the inner view. Those with the greatest realization of the profound inner nature are most able to transform the mundane world into a mandala of deities in which the saving action of the buddhas radiates eternally.

Tantric Yoga

Another major strand of tantric meditation practices is the use of subtle energy flows in the human body in the cultivation of enlightened mind. Yogic techniques for control of physical energies and generation of mental stability had long been used by buddhist meditators. Practiced by ascetics, renunciants, and meditators of many traditions, various forms of breath control, physical exercise and austerities, and imaginative concentration on internal bodily processes were familiar elements of spiritual practice at the time of Shakyamuni Buddha. They were among the practices explored by Siddhartha in his quest for enlightenment, and over time they were incorporated into various forms of buddhist meditation. As with all buddhist practice, the goal of physical yoga was always the realization of selflessness and the removal of mental obscurations that hide the ultimate inner nature from the mind's view.

The impact of tantric yoga on the cultivation of bodhichitta is grounded in the unity of the mental and physical parts of the human being. Although the nature of consciousness eludes definition, human beings obviously comprise both a physical organism and a subjective awareness. The energies of feelings and ideas coexist with the energies of tissues and organs such that there can be no absolute distinction between body and mind in any organism. In a conscious being there is a reciprocity of influence between matter and mind. Tantric yoga recognizes this and unites the energies of mentation with those of bodily existence in creating techniques for bringing the fundamental nature of mind to conscious awareness.

As the third turning of buddhist doctrine evolved, with its emphases on direct experience of the inner nature and on making use of all the sensory and functional resources of the body-mind complex, vajrayana practitioners included the yogic manipulation of inner energies in their teachings and meditation.

The states of energy that occur and fluctuate within the organs of the body produce changing patterns that manifest at every level of human life: from the molecular level to the level of conscious action, and on to the interpersonal and cultural dimensions of our lives. The natural processes of the body – such as breathing, eating, perceiving, thinking, and acting – and the ordinary functioning of the physiological systems – such as the circulatory, endocrine, nervous, and reproductive systems – generate energy fields and flows that are constantly active accompaniments to all of our physical and mental actions. Repetitive patterns of energy flow, like ocean currents or tides, condition mental and physical experience, predisposing people to different kinds of emotional, intellectual, and material experiences at different times. The essential point is that differing states of bodily energy produce differing mental states, and different states of mind produce different states of energy in the body and its organ systems.

The subtle body that is addressed in tantric yoga consists generally of certain patterns of moving energy within the physical organs, bodies, and surrounding spaces of human beings. Individuals may be variably more or less aware of these energy fields and flows; and through intensive training such as that practiced by tantric yogis, they may gain greater awareness of their bodily energies as well as some degree of conscious control over the organic processes involved.

In tantric yoga the elemental biological energy of human beings is identified as prana, a word also signifying breath, wind, and life force. The movements of energy in the human body and consciousness are said to be the movements of prana. States of mind are said to correspond to the internal conditions of prana within the individual. Prana is imagined to flow continuously through a subtle network of incorporeal channels, called nadis, that permeate the body. There is a central channel running in front of the spinal cord, from the abdomen to the brain. On either side of the central channel are two smaller channels which open into the nostrils and join the central channel below the navel. These main channels are connected to a nerve-like network of smaller channels spreading throughout the body. Major nodes of this network, called chakras, are located along the central channel. There are chakras at the reproductive organs, the navel, the heart, the throat, the inner brain, and the upper brain, with different traditions using somewhat different descriptions.

The prana energy is often conceived as being concentrated in two small spheres, drops, or seeds, one white and one red, called bindus, that correspond symbolically to various fundamental biological polarities such as male and female, sperm and egg, active and passive, and so forth. In tantric meditation the meditator controls and circulates such energies as breath, heat, and mental imagery in order to influence the movement of prana and the pranic essences through the nadis of his body.

The mutual correspondence and reciprocity of mind and prana is a fundamental principle of tantric yoga. When the energy currents are peaceful, harmonious, and balanced, the nature of the inner mind is more accessible to consciousness. When, on the contrary, personal energy flows are violent, conflicting, or unbalanced, insight into the inner mind becomes more difficult. A calm and recollected mind tends to generate calm and harmonious bodily energies, which in turn contribute to the stability and clarity of the inner view.

According to tantric teachings, the psychophysical energy of prana usually moves chaotically through the nadis and chakras. In tantric meditation the prana and the bindus are caused to move harmoniously through the central channel so as to unite their different essences and actions in revealing to the practitioner the full nature of the inner mind.

Tantric yoga offers creative possibilities to those on the bodhisattva path who have understood well the emptiness and luminosity of the inner mind and who have deeply realized the meaning of the six selfless perfections. As with most vajrayana practices, meditation on the subtle energy body and its transformations must generally be carried out under the guidance of a wise guru inbued with great virtue, skill, and insight.

The Mandala of the Five Buddhas

The genius of the vajrayana is epitomized by the Mandala of the Five Buddhas, sometimes referred to as the Five Buddha Families. The Mandala of the Five Buddhas is a symbolic paradigm expressing the inner unity of all states of mind and indicating how negative and harmful mental states can be transformed into positive and and beneficial ones. The teachings on the Five Buddhas recognize that the formless inner mind is the originator of all thoughts and experience. All forms of understanding and all forms of ignorance are fundamentally equivalent in the emptiness of ultimate truth – the simple, universal reality called buddha nature, the dharmakaya, the uncreated, and so forth. The occurrence of basic, nonconceptual awareness is the common source of all forms of consciousness.

Though, relatively speaking, positive and negative actions always produce corresponding results, in the absolute realm of unconditional awareness there are no judgments, words, or descriptions. The energy producing ignorance is also the energy producing wisdom. When the mind encounters its inner nature, illusions and errors tend to dissolve and the qualities of the enlightened nature appear.

The Mandala of the Five Buddhas consists visually of a central buddha surrounded by four other buddhas. Each buddha represents one of the five skandhas of buddhist psychology (form, feelings, perceptions, mental formations, and consciousness), one of the cardinal vices or mental afflictions (attachment, aversion, ignorance, pride, and envy), one of the five physical elements of traditional metaphysics (earth, water, air, fire, and space), and one of five aspects of the transcendent wisdom realized with the awakening to buddha nature. Each buddha is said to symbolize or generate a buddhafield containing a large family of buddhas, bodhisattvas, yidams, dharma protectors, and other enlightened inhabitants. The Five Buddhas display particular mudras (hand gestures) and are accompanied by other symbols of their qualities and activities. Depending on the complexity of the visualizations imagined, each of the Five Buddhas may be envisioned in union with a yidam consort representing additional aspects of the cosmos and the nature of inner wisdom. Elaborate iconographies have evolved in various practice traditions assigning somewhat different names, colors, ideas, and other symbolical associations to each of the buddha families and positions of the mandala.

In general, the buddha families represent different characteristic patterns of thought, insight, delusion, and activity exhibited by different individuals. The transformative power of the mandala is grounded in the fundamental insight that the essential nature of pure awareness is enlightened wisdom. All of the forms of ignorance or delusion symbolized by the mandala are the nature of all human beings; and all of the forms of wisdom and virtue symbolized by the five buddhas are likewise the essential nature of all beings. The entire mandala with all of its potentialities is seen as the true nature of every person.

According to a common version of the mandala, the central position is occupied by Buddha Vairochana. Vairochana represents the skandha of form and the physical element of space. The delusion associated with the center of the mandala is the fundamental ignorance existing everywhere that mind fails to understand the ultimate nature of reality.

Vairochana represents the universal wisdom that is the very nature of the dharmakaya, the essence of all things. Vairochana signifies that the inner nature of psychic confusion and delusion is none other than the enlightened awareness of the buddhas. When this is fully realized by the practitioner, the ignorance disappears, revealing the all-knowing mind of the buddha.

The buddhas of the four directions around the center represent the major vices of consciousness and alternative antidotes to them, as modeled by the buddhas who have overcome the vices and realized the transcendent virtues of their accomplishments. In the east is the Buddha Akshobya, representing the skandha of consciousness and the element of water. Akshobya is the transformation of the delusions of hatred, anger, and aversion. He symbolizes the mirror-like wisdom of the enlightened mind, which reflects all things to consciousness exactly as they appear.

In the south is the Buddha Ratnasambhava, representing the skandha of feeling and the element of earth. Ratnasambhava symbolizes the affliction of pride and the equalizing wisdom that apprehends the ultimate equality of all things.

In the west is the Buddha Amitabha, representing the skandha of perception and the element of fire. Amitabha symbolizes the delusions of desire and attachment. His wisdom is the discriminating wisdom by which all perceptual and conceptual distinctions are known and understood.

In the north is the Buddha Amoghasiddhi, representing the skandha of formation (will) and the element of air. Amoghasiddhi symbolizes the afflictions of envy and jealousy. His wisdom is the all-accomplishing wisdom that achieves all things.

The unity of confusion and understanding symbolized by the Five Buddhas is rooted in the living experience of consciousness. Self-awareness, the elemental mental reality, gives rise, through the steps of dependent origination, to the formations of conceptual thought and motivation. When these processes lead to belief in the ultimate reality of passing ideas, it is the beginning of confusion and misunderstanding. The Mandala of the Five Buddhas demonstrates that all forms of misunderstanding arise with a means of dispelling the confusion.

The means of clarification is the inner mind of awareness from which all thoughts originate. When the thinking mind turns its attention to the starting point of ideas, it becomes possible to reorient consciousness to different points of view. The full experience of selflessness destroys all negative states of mind. Delving deeply into the vices of consciousness, one finds that as they dissipate, new realities may emerge, such as the buddhafields of the five buddhas.

The open mind of inner awareness is free from all conceptual limitations. Liberated from self-centered ideas, the mind can become the enlightenment of a buddha. The Mandala of the Five Buddhas points the way to profound re-direction of the apparent personality. Those who actualize the mandala in their lives realize the wisdoms of the five buddhas and perform their compassionate actions.

The direct approach of the third dharma turning encourages people to cut straight to the heart of their mental confusion and immediately abandon it in the same movement of attention that recognizes the enduring inner nature.

The Five Buddhas should be understood as different aspects of a unitary reality. Realizing any of the five wisdoms brings liberation from ignorance and confusion. The mirror-like wisdom of Akshobya allows one to know exactly what occurs and when it happens. The equalizing wisdom of Ratnasambhava sees the sameness of all things. The discriminating wisdom of Amitabha understands all the differences among ideas and experiences. The all-accomplishing wisdom of Amoghasiddhi overcomes all obstacles and brings all activities to perfect fulfillment. The universal wisdom of Vairochana draws from every experience the profound inner reality of buddha nature.

The Mandala of the Five Buddhas symbolizes the basic mechanisms of consciousness giving rise to both ignorance and understanding, evil as well as virtue; and it indicates effective means by which the mind can be purified of its errors and recognized as the ultimate beacon of truth. All forms of ignorance originate in the mistaking of mental appearances for unconditional realities. All forms of wisdom require an interruption in the causal chains of conceptual delusion. When consciousness escapes its conceptual bonds and regains its naturally pure awareness, it discovers the inner source of all ideas, appearances, and understanding. Then the providential nature of the dharmakaya will appear.

Coemergence of Mind and Appearances

The experience of the inner mind is always available to consciousness. The "right understanding" of mental and sensory phenomena that can be realized through selfless insight is the permanent condition of the inner mind. The buddhadharma has always aimed at revealing this universal inner reality to all. The many forms of practice developed in the three cycles of dharma teachings, and in all their profound elaborations up to the present, have been designed to spread this sort of understanding.

A popular representation of the ultimate understanding in buddhist philosophy is of a permanent inner awareness that sees both the manifestations of sensory and conceptual experience and the fundamental inner mind nature as emerging simultaneously from consciousness in every moment. It is the basic nature of mind to manifest emptiness and cognitive lucidity (awareness) at all times, while also revealing to sentient beings all the appearances that conscious perception produces. The world that presents itself to human consciousness consists always of both the formless inner reality and the interlinked conceptual appearances that arise in the space of inner awareness.

Buddhist teachers often describe the experience of inner emptiness as experiencing mind in stillness. In contrast to this bare, nonconceptual awareness, the experience of thought and sensation is described as experiencing mind in movement. These metaphors encourage the view that the empty inner mind, on the one hand, and its conceptions and productions, on the other, are different but complementary aspects of the same thing. The mind's nature is not changed as it shifts between thought and mental stillness. Both the moving mind and the still mind can be conceptualized endlessly, prolonging the motion almost forever. But the nonconceptual inner essence is always active and self-aware, and it can know itself in the midst of any mental movement, however insistent, excruciating, or inexpressible.

The fundamental, nonconceptual mind of emptiness and pure awareness gives rise to the conceptual experiences of the outer mind as a fire gives rise to light. As the fire and its light cannot be separated, phenomenal experiences cannot be separated from the inner awareness in which they originate. The transcendent world of enlightenment and the phenomenal world of appearances are different manifestations of the same world. That which is called nirvana is none other than that which is called samsara. The ordinary mind of ordinary life is the infinite mind of enlightened awareness.

The most exalted teachings of the third turning describe the simultaneous coexistence of the inner nature and phenomenal experience as coemergence or co-origination. Both aspects of the mind arise together, as a unity. The inseparability of the empty inner awareness and the appearances of conscious experience is said to be the basic nature of reality. This constant but ever-changing reality is identified by the words dharmakaya, buddha nature, original mind, and so forth. It is the fundamental nature of all mind and experience, including everything considered to be ignorance and everything considered to be enlightenment.

Verbal and conceptual descriptions, however, should never be mistaken for complete understanding. As emphasized in all of the mahayana wisdom teachings, the ultimate nature of mind and appearances that is described as emptiness or interdependence is beyond existence and non-existence. Although it can be experienced in any moment of consciousness, it cannot be grasped or defined by the intellect, and it is constantly disappearing into the next moment. The ultimate inconceivability of the mind gives rise to the paradoxical terminology of the mahayana according to which mind and all of its fleeting manifestations are said neither to exist nor not to exist, or to be beyond any characterization whatever. From before Shakyamuni until now, no one has been able to reduce the vast, formless experience of pure consciousness to the arbitrary limitations of human language.

The third cycle of the Buddha's teachings expanded understanding of the mind by emphasizing the continuity of inner awareness through all the changes of consciousness. The teachings on the coemergence of mind and appearances express the essence of the third turning and provide a direct means of attaining full realization of the mind's inner nature.

The buddhist path has often been summarized as a matter of view, meditation, and action. A correct understanding of the general nature of experience is to be combined with careful meditation practice to produce the realization and activity of the bodhisattvas. The vajrayana tradition of coemergent wisdom is often taught as a similar practice sequence described as ground, path, and fruition. The ground is the fundamental nature of mind and experience, what can be called reality. The path is the means by which this reality is brought to conscious realization, consisting mainly of the meditation practices revealing the inner nature, but implying also all the skillful means contributing to this accomplishment. The fruition is the full realization of the ground reality within the human mind, with the full display in human behavior of all its enlightened qualities and actions.

Meditation practices in which traditional techniques for generating tranquility and insight are combined to reveal the ground and produce the fruits of ultimate realization are taught in several vajrayana traditions. In general, the essence of these practices is to experience the basic inner state directly and without distraction or mental fabrication for periods of focused yet relaxed and open awareness. The meditator attempts to rest mindfully, but without intellectualization or dualistic separation, in the bare present awareness of the inner mind. The mental focus is only on maintaining silent interior awareness of what the mind is doing *right now.* Gradually, through pursuing this meditation diligently over time, the meditator gains greater clarity and certainty about the nature of his mind and its projections.

A traditional analysis presenting the coemergent path to full realization of the ground reality divides the path into four yogas or stages: (1) the yoga of one-pointedness, by which the mind is brought to stable concentration on, and awareness of, the instantaneous inner nature; (2) the yoga of simplicity, by which the mind is brought to non-conceptual awareness that lucid emptiness is the ultimate nature of both the mind and its appearances; (3) the yoga of one taste, by which the mind is brought to the realization that all the multitudinous appearances it experiences are only its same and single nature; and (4) the yoga of non-meditation, in which the mind has so fully realized its coemergent nature that all ignorance and mental confusion disappear and the pure selfless awareness and action of enlightenment manifest spontaneously and continuously with all experience of consciousness.

It is said that these meditations result in a mind capable of knowing the perfectly pure inner awareness within any conceptual or phenomenal experience. Bodhisattvas who have attained such realizations are said to experience the self-liberation of appearances, whereby ordinary phenomena are transformed into perfect wisdom, or the natural perfection of the inner mind. These realizations are the nature of ultimate bodhichitta, the primordial understanding of consciousness at the heart of the Buddha's enlightenment and his wordless transmission to all the generations of his successors. The fruition resulting from these practices and realizations is the projection through history of the supreme wisdom and activity of the enlightened ones.

Vajrayana practitioners engaging in tantric meditation and the meditations on coemergent wisdom are generally required to pursue extensive preliminary meditation and devotional practices in order to train themselves in the disciplines and aptitudes necessary for advanced practice. Securing the guidance of accomplished gurus or spiritual friends is another basic necessity. Though it is often said that ultimately the mind itself is the preeminent guru, the boundless generosity and power of the devoted sangha community is an indispensable resource for anyone wishing to pursue the most serious forms of dharma practice in any of the practice traditions.

The Appendix contains two examples of profound dharma instructions imparted by realized masters in the coemergent wisdom tradition: "The Dharma of Mahamudra According to Maitripa, as Told by Marpa" and a contemporary verse from Khenpo Tsultrim Gyamtso Rinpoche.

Wise and Skillful Living: the Middle Way

The practice of buddhadharma, of which this is only a very imperfect summary, comprises a vast history in which people of many lands and times have sought to realize their inner nature and overcome the fundamental misunderstandings and dissatisfactions generated by conscious life. The three cycles of dharma teachings address different aspects of the mental confusions that have always veiled the inner nature from self-awareness. Of the many teachings and practices available in the various buddhist traditions, some are more suitable and effective than others for particular persons. It is traditionally taught that the Buddha provided 84,000 sets of dharma teachings, corresponding to 84,000 kinds of mental confusion to which beings are subject.

The mental obscurations that interfere with recognition of the true inner nature operate as outlined in the chain of dependent origination. From rudimentary self-awareness, one imagines a dualistic separation of the world into ideas of self and other, followed by the development of thought and action strategies to protect and gratify the subjective self, and to control the surrounding world. The mental reactions that obscure the buddha nature are often said to be of three general kinds: disturbing emotions, mistaken "knowledge," and habitual patterns of thought. They all stem from conceptual mistakes that condition the outer mind to false or inadequate interpretations of experience.

The central impetus of buddhadharma is to encourage all persons to live mindfully, becoming ever more aware of the inner realities of their minds and of the causal sequences producing their thoughts and experiences. Persistent attentiveness to one's mental and external actions leads to understanding of the patterns of causation or karma by which one's personal experience is constructed. Karma, it will be found, is both freeing and binding. As beliefs imputing inherent existence to temporary and conditional experiences lead step by step to disturbing emotions and counterproductive efforts to force the world to conform to our delusions, so also gaining insight into the selfless inner nature and increasing mindfulness of mental phenomena lead us step by step to liberation from conceptual errors and ultimately to the fruits of enlightenment.

As people pursue the noble eightfold path, cultivate bodhichitta, and accomplish the six perfections, they will come to experience the profound benefits of realizing selfless wisdom and compassion. Those who diligently practice the meditations that pacify and illuminate their minds will eventually come to realize the coemergence of the unconditional inner truth with the myriad of conditional appearances constantly projected from the inner awareness as inexorably as waves rising continuously from the global ocean.

The karmic causes leading from ignorance to enlightenment are often summarized as being two accumulations, the accumulation of merit and the accumulation of wisdom. Merit is accumulated through virtuous conduct and diligent performance of meditation and devotional practices bringing the blessings of skillful and compassionate action to the practitioner. Wisdom is accumulated through repeated exposure of the self-aware consciousness to its own inner nature, with gradual diminution of the conceptual overlays and assumptions that mislead the mind into constructing imaginary ideas about itself.

The central gift of Siddhartha's dharma is the knowledge that the miseries of ordinary life can be overcome by careful attention to the inner essence of the ordinary mind, combined with earnest effort to bring one's behavior into harmony with the resulting realizations. Discovering that an impersonal, unidentifiable, empty awareness is the core of all consciousness, one finds that impulses toward selfish and harmful behavior are replaced with selfless compassion and the energy to put that compassion into action preventing and relieving the sufferings of others. The practices taught by Shakyamuni and his successors for the development and implementation of these insights range from the very simple to the very complex, always emphasizing cultivation of wisdom as to the nature of mind and engagement in skillful and benevolent action in the course of daily life.

Buddhist ethical admonitions can all be derived from the compassion inherent in the wisdom of selflessness. That is why the perfection of wisdom is called the mother of all the buddhas. A few common guidelines for the conduct of practitioners illustrate the practicality and profundity of the moral dimensions of buddhadharma. There are said to be three poisons that are the root of all evil: ignorance, attachment, and aversion. This fundamental set of cardinal vices is sometimes expanded to include pride and envy, as in the mandala of the five buddhas. However one categorizes the mistakes of thought and action, it is clear that they all begin with ignorance of the true inner nature and the setting up of an imaginary self to be hurt or helped by circumstances.

Another simple but profound formula of practical advice is to beware of the influence of the eight worldly winds, sometimes called the eight worldly dharmas. These dangerous winds are the four pairs: gain and loss; pleasure and pain; praise and blame; fame and obscurity. Buddhists are advised to avoid being motivated or blown about by any of these eight winds.

Shakyamuni's dharma is taught as a Middle Way between conceptual polarities. This reflects the fundamental interdependence, relativity, or emptiness of ideas and experiences; but it also serves as a broad guideline for moderation in moral judgments. One trying to identify a standard of moral conduct in terms of opposing behavioral alternatives will often be able to do no better than resolve to do neither too much of "this" nor too much of "that," or some of "this" and some of "that." Advocating the avoidance of extremes in philosophical analysis as well as in the decisions of daily life, the Middle Way points its followers toward lives of intellectual, emotional, and physical balance.

However one resolves moral challenges and dilemmas, or other decisional issues, the buddhadharma always focuses attention on the causal consequences of willful choices. However much one's experiences are shaped by the effects of past causes, whether his doing or not, when one learns ways to correct conceptual and volitional mistakes he has made, the future becomes subject to his freedom of choice. In the dynamics of karmic causation, we can be responsible for our own enlightenment as well as for the continuation of our habitual delusions.

As buddhist practitioners follow the dharma path, gradually gaining the wisdom of self-knowledge and improving the qualities of their actions of body, speech, and mind, they approach ever closer to the ideal of enlightenment. Learning to live simple, straightforward, happy lives free of obsessions and stubborn beliefs, yet steeped in sensible compassion, moral conduct, and vigilant mindfulness, they will deepen and extend their wordless awareness of the unchanging, self-luminous inner nature of ordinary mind. As they become more familiar with the selfless inner mind shining constantly throughout the kaleidoscopic changes of conceptual consciousness, they will identify their lives more with the formless inner light and less with the dreamlike images of sensory and conceptual experience, until they reach an instinctive appreciation of the coemergent identity of the appearances and the inner light.

Since insight into the buddha nature is an interior experience, its accomplishment by one person generally cannot be known directly by anyone else. Buddhist teachers advise that enlightenment can be indicated by the superior qualities and activities of highly realized practitioners, by the extraordinarily selfless and virtuous behavior exhibited by such men and women. It is also said that persons of great inner realization can recognize intuitively such realization in others.

Concepts like enlightenment, emptiness, and inner truth are always potentially misleading because they are verbal symbols attached to a transcendent reality that is beyond exact conception or description. The underlying inner nature cannot be modified by thinking or speaking about it. Ideas about it cannot add anything to it or subtract anything from it. So words and ideas, if they are not to obscure the inner vision, must be allowed to come to rest when the conscious mind contemplates its pure innate awareness. When conceptualization resumes, the meditator who has experienced the inner reality will know the thinking to be the movement of the inner source.

The emptiness of inherent existence that is the hallmark of the conceptual world in the buddhist view naturally applies to the conceptions of buddhadharma as well as to other thoughts and sensations. All words and ideas are at most conditional interpretations of indeterminable experiences. Accordingly practitioners are always exhorted not to cling to ideas of emptiness, buddha nature, or other dharma truths. Shakyamuni Buddha taught that even wisdom and virtue are to be abandoned when their purposes have been achieved, as a raft is left on a riverbank after it has carried a passenger across the water. The sutras record that the final words of the Great Sage, as his material existence ended, were these: "All dharmas are impermanent. Strive diligently for understanding."

This "Summary of Buddhadharma" was compiled for his friends by a dharma student having confidence in the buddhist path but little knowledge of the depths of its teachings and even less realization of the results of diligent practice. Those seeking more information on the way of buddhadharma are advised to consult the sutras, the authoritative commentaries, and other respected texts of the three vehicles, and the dharma teachings of realized masters whose qualities and activities confirm the authenticity of their wisdom and skill.

May all beings awaken to inner peace.

Appendix

1. The Bodhisattva Vow

Until I reach the heart of Enlightenment, I take refuge in all the Buddhas, in the Dharma, and in the assembly of Bodhisattvas.

Just as the former Sugatas generated the Bodhichitta and passed through all the levels, stage by stage, of a Bodhisattva's training, likewise, in order to benefit beings, I too generate the Bodhichitta, and will follow the training, stage by stage, in the same manner.

(Recite three times.)

Now my life is bearing fruit. Having obtained an excellent human existence, I have now taken birth in the Buddha race, so that I have become a Buddha's son [*or* daughter]. Therefore, now I will do nothing other than what accords with this affiliation, so that this noble and flawless lineage does not become sullied.

Today I invite all beings to enjoy happiness in the presence of all those in whom I take refuge until they reach Buddhahood itself. May all beings rejoice.

Where the precious Bodhichitta has not arisen, may it arise; where it has arisen, may it never diminish, but go on increasing more and more. Being inseparable from the Bodhichitta, may I strive to practice the Bodhisattva Conduct, and, being in the secure hold of all the Buddhas, may I abandon all evils.

May all that the Bodhisattvas are wishing for the benefit of beings be accomplished, and may all beings receive the happiness that the Lords have in mind for them. May all beings become happy. May all lower existences be emptied forever. May all the prayers of resolute aspiration made by the Bodhisattvas of whatever level be accomplished.

Note: "Sugata" is another word for Buddha, meaning approximately "Well-Gone One."

This form of the Bodhisattva Vow is a variation of one provided by Karma Triyana Dharmachakra Monastery, Woodstock, New York, in 1986.

2. A Verse of Soen Nakagawa Roshi

Realizing at last
this world and that other
are not two,
I pick flowers in Spring.

This verse was quoted by Eido Shimano Roshi in a remembrance of Soen Nakagawa Roshi published in the Vajradhatu Sun, Vol. 6, No. 6 (August-September, 1984), p. 1.

3. A Verse from the Diamond Sutra

Thus shall you think of all this fleeting world:
a star at dawn, a bubble in a stream,
a flash of lightning in a summer cloud,
a flickering lamp, a phantom, and a dream.

From *The Diamond Sutra and The Sutra of Hui Neng*, translated by A. F. Price and Wong Mou-Lam (Boulder: Shambhala Publications, Inc., 1969), p. 74. For this volume The Diamond Sutra was translated by A. F. Price. The quoted verse, however, is the translation of Dr. Kenneth Saunders, as Mr. Price notes where it appears, at the end of the sutra.

4. The Dharma of Mahamudra According to Maitripa, as Told by Marpa

The Dharma of Mahamudra
According to Maitripa, as told by Marpa

Outer grasping, the appearance of sense objects,
continuously flows as great bliss.
Realize it as unborn dharmakaya.

Inner fixation, the mind-consciousness,
is discursive, which cannot be grasped as real.
Therefore see it as naked insight
without foundation.

Generally, all dharmas of apparent existence
are primordially nonexistent and unborn.
Realize them as the essence of simplicity.

Do not desire to abandon samsara,
and there is no nirvana to attain.

Samsara and nirvana are the self-
liberated innate state.
Realize this unity as great bliss.

Even if you emptied out the minds of
the buddhas of the three times,
there is nothing more ultimate than this.

From *The Life of Marpa the Translator*, by Tsang Nyön Heruka, translated by the Nalanda Translation Committee under the direction of Chögyam Trungpa (Boulder: Prajñā Press, 1982; reprinted Boston: Shambhala Publications, Inc., 1995), pp. 113-114. The title was supplied by the compiler.

5. A Verse of Khenpo Tsultrim Gyamtso Rinpoche

Realizing mind's true nature is the view,
Resting in this true nature is meditation,
Letting thoughts of hope and fear dissolve is the fruition.
So know the true nature of your mind well.
Phenomena are appearance-emptiness, like rainbows.
When you are not attached to them, they are self-liberated.
Whatever of samsara's happiness or suffering may arise,
When you are not attached to it, samsara is self-liberated.
Of all things to seek, self-liberated openness is supreme,
So within self-liberated openness, let go and relax.
Find your rest in self-liberated openness.

Email provided by Ari Goldfield for the students of Khenpo Tsultrim Gyamtso Rinpoche, November 28, 2009.

6. The Last Words of Shakyamuni Buddha

> All dharmas are impermanent. Strive diligently for understanding.

A compilation and interpretation of various translations from the Pali Canon.

Notes on the Illustrations

1. The illustration on the cover and at the beginning of Part One is a contemporary interpretation of a dharmachakra or dharma wheel, a traditional symbol of buddhadharma. It was drawn by Luisa Restrepo from a design of Michael Wolf. Ms. Restrepo can be reached at Triple 1 Studio, Baton Rouge, La., www.triple1studio.com, 1triplestudio@gmail.com.

2. The frontispiece, which is repeated in the Appendix, is an image of Shakyamuni Buddha in the dharmachakra or teaching mudra, drawn by Luisa Restrepo. It is based on a traditional woodblock print reproduced in *Tibetan and Himalayan Woodblock Prints* by Douglas Weiner (New York: Dover Publications, Inc., 1974) as Print No. 1.

3. The drawing at the beginning of Part Two, showing a jewel in a lotus presented by a Buddha hand, was created by Luisa Restrepo after a concept of Michael Wolf.

4. The illustration at the beginning of Part Three is an image of the yidam Vajrasattva, a name signifying "indestructible being." Vajrasattva symbolizes the eternal realities of Buddha Nature and their purifying action upon the human mind. The illustration was drawn by Luisa Restrepo.

It is based on a traditional woodblock print reproduced in *Tibetan and Himalayan Woodblock Prints* by Douglas Weiner (New York: Dover Publications, Inc., 1974) as Print No. 39.

Made in the USA
Charleston, SC
10 November 2015